Roman Jakobson and Beyond: Language as a System of Signs

JANUA
LINGUARUM   Series Maior 109
Studia Memoriae
Nicolai van Wijk Dedicata

edenda curat
C. H. van Schooneveld
Indiana University

Roman Jakobson and Beyond: Language as a System of Signs

The Quest for the Ultimate Invariants in Language

Rodney B. Sangster

Mouton Publishers
Berlin · New York · Amsterdam

Rodney B. Sangster
Indiana University

ISBN 90 279 3040 6

lej 2-15-85

To Ray and Iwona

Contents

Preface

Introduction   Language as a System of Signs   3

Chapter one   Phonology   9

1. The sign principle as applied to the structure of sound   9
2. The phoneme   12
3. Invariance at the level of distinctive features   18

Chapter two   Morphophonemics   29

1. Definition and scope of the subject   29
2. The structure and functions of alternations   32
3. Other formal devices in morphology   42

Chapter three   Morphology   47

1. The sign principle as applied to the structure of meaning   47
2. Introduction to grammatical meaning: The Russian case system   54
3. Structural differences between phonological and morphological oppositions   62

4. Extension of the analysis: the system
    of Russian prepositions and preverbs   79
5. Transition to lexical meaning   104

Chapter four   Syntax   113

1. The semantics of syntax   113
2. Adjectival and adverbial modification
    in English, French and Russian   114
3. A semantic appreciation of
    government and agreement   133

Chapter five   Meaning in Perspective   141

1. Abstractness, invariance, and the
    definition of semantic features   141
2. The role of deixis in semantics:
    Meaning as perception   155
3. Sign theory and semantic universals   163
4. The place of syntax in the sign
    theory of language   171

Notes   183

Bibliography   195

Index   203

Preface

The primary aim of this volume is to present a complete over-
view of the theoretical and methodological principles of linguistic sign theory, and their consequences for linguistic research.
The specific approach adopted is one which is held in common
by two leading world linguists and Slavists, Roman Jakobson
and C.H. van Schooneveld. What unites the work of these two
scholars and provides the guiding principle of this study is the
conviction that meaning is inherent in linguistic form, so that
we cannot investigate the properties of either domain (form or
meaning) without making constant and direct reference to the
properties of the other. Such a view of language realizes that
surface linguistic forms are much more revealing of their semantic content than is generally assumed in the current state of linguistic science, and that they in fact provide a wealth of evidence
for the construction of semantic theory, which is the major subject of this study. One of the most important results of this
analysis will be establishment of a theory of MEANING AS
PERCEPTION which for the first time allows us to specify the
locus of linguistic meaning, without having recourse to an un-
verifiable concept of mind. Neither imprisoned within the structure of language nor divorced from it by being defined on objects
in the external world, meaning is defined here as the structuration
of acts of perception given direct formal expression through
vocalization. Perhaps the major achievement of this approach lies
in the resolution it provides for the perennial problem of structural linguistics, that of relating linguistic structures to the phenomena in other domains upon which linguistics obviously im-

pinges, especially the world of events and things, communication about which is the primary function of language.

I would not have written this book if I did not think that it would provide, in addition to an outline of a particular philosophy of language, specific solutions to some of the major problems of current linguistic research, in phonology and syntax as well as in morphology. For example, treating formal linguistic elements as directly reflective of their informational content will also provide explicit definitions and justifications for a complete hierarchy of distinct, **relatively** autonomous levels of linguistic structure, and of the abstract units which comprise these levels. A difficulty does arise in this respect, however, and that is how to establish a common ground upon which to engage in meaningful dialogue with colleagues holding substantively different points of view. The problematics of communication in the field of linguistics are rather severe, due not so much to personalities as to the fact that linguistic science still lacks a generally accepted definition of its primary subject — language. And there remains even greater disagreement as to what the goals of linguistic theory ought to be. But there is more of a common ground when it comes to determining what the issues are that linguistic theory should address, and with this in mind I have made every effort to talk directly to the issues themselves, rather than to argue solely in terms of a particular theory. Specifically, I have tried to aim my arguments at concerns that have dominated current controversies in linguistics, and to identify all the facts that pertain to the issues in question, not limiting myself to those aspects that are of importance in any one theory.

In this context one of my primary concerns has been to dispel some of the myths about so-called structuralism with respect to a broad range of issues in phonology, morphology, and syntax. One misconception is that the structuralist approach necessarily leads to the establishment of a closed (sui generis) system of language, which I alluded to above. Another involves the frequent implication that European and American structuralists share an essentially taxonomic approach to language, which has had particularly important consequences for phonological research. In arguments against the phoneme as a distinct sound unit, for example, only those aspects of the issue which lend themselves to criticisms of taxonomic phonemics, such as linearity and bi-uniqueness, have been presented. No one to my knowledge has ever disputed Jakobson's substantive reasons for insisting upon a separate, relatively autonomous phonemic level, which have little to do with taxonomies per se. The issue of whether or not there is justification for such a level has thus been obscured by limiting the arguments to just those that concern the distributional aspects of phonology. If it could be shown that Jakobson's approach, which recognizes the informational function of all linguistic forms, explains a range of facts that are not accounted for in any explicit way in a purely formal phonology — namely, facts about the distinct role of the addressee in the speech chain, certain psychologically relevant facts about sound discrimination, and so forth — and at the same time provides a completely natural solution to the current problem of how abstract are phonological elements, then there is every reason to reconsider the validity of a separate phonemic level. This is precisely what I try to establish in Chapter 1, where I present in detail Jakobson's observations on the essence of phonological elements. I follow his reasoning closely, some might say tediously, but I do so in order to insure that all the arguments that pertain to this issue are fully presented and documented.

The conclusions drawn in Chapter 1 provide the basis for a discussion of morphophonemics in Chapter 2, which contains a definitive statement on the dual nature of alternations, and defines the boundary between phonology and morphology. The argumentation here again follows Jakobson, whose work has unquestionably provided the most eloquent expression of the issues involved in distinguishing between these levels. The first two chapters, then, are largely retrospective, but still indispensable in a text such as this, one of whose primary motivations is to demonstrate the theoretical consistency of the approach being taken at all levels of analysis.

Chapter 3 initiates the discussion of semantics proper, which is critical to our understanding of the essence of formal elements in both morphology and syntax. Once more the approach derives from Jakobson the statement of its fundamental principles, but the argumentation evolves beyond Jakobson at the point where lexical meaning comes into consideration. Here the work of van Schooneveld plays a central role, and his contribution to semantic theory is fully elaborated. The subsequent discussions of semantics in syntax (Chapter 4) and of the general issues that are considered in Chapter 5 owe a great deal to van Schooneveld's persistent search for the semantic essence of all linguistic elements, while the development of the reasoning in these later chapters remains my own. Because of the special nature of Chapter 5, where the theory of meaning as perception and the outlines for a semantically based theory of syntax are presented, some readers may wish to look at this final chapter first to see where the approach ultimately leads, though I would caution that many of the points made there depend on assumptions justified and supported only in the preceding chapters.

No doubt some readers will be put off by the lack of formalization of some of the solutions presented here, especially given the present climate of linguistic research, where formalization of grammars has assumed a dominant role in theory construction and motivation. My response on this point derives from the dictates of linguistic sign theory itself, which seeks the primary motivation of all linguistic structures in their semantic essence. Determination of the nature of a mechanical device that would generate such structures is thus necessarily of secondary importance in such a theory. This is not to say, however, that the nature of these devices is irrelevant to linguistic analysis, but only that concern for this aspect of the investigation is not allowed to dominate or to become the primary motivation of the inquiry. Otherwise the nature of the devices themselves tends to dictate where we look for solutions to linguistic problems, and even, as I have already noted, how we define the issues. Such a situation is, in my opinion, especially dangerous in the present state of linguistic science, where unanimity on such basic matters as the definition of fundamental terms still has not been achieved. Formalization of the solutions suggested here, especially in the sections on syntax, is the subject of intensive, on-going research.

Another factor that will no doubt have an impact upon the appreciation of this study by different readers is the extent to which the data presented are drawn from Russian. This is especially true of the section on morphology, where the principles and methods of semantic analysis are initially elaborated. To those not familiar with Russian or other Slavic languages I can only say that the establishment of a set of conceptual features as sophisticated as the ones required by this kind of analysis demands a great deal of time, more than has been available to treat a variety of languages to the degree necessary for presentation in a study such as this. On the other hand, Slavists and others who know the subtleties of the Russian language well may feel that not enough data from Russian has been provided to make the arguments always convincing. With them I might agree, but I would also add that my intention has been to find a middle ground between a highly data-oriented study and a purely theoretical treatise, so that the audience for this book can be both general linguists and Slavists at the same time.

Several people have contributed in one way or another to this book. Above all there is Cornelis van Schooneveld, mentor, colleague, and friend, for whom a form without meaning is like a sea without water. His remarkable eye for meaning has given the quest for invariance an entirely new dimension. Roman Jakobson's personal involvement with the early stages of this work was instrumental in giving it direction, and his writings have always proven to be an endless source of inspiration. Charles Townsend's concern and friendship over the years have been most valuable and appreciated, and his careful reading of the manuscript provided a much needed perspective that led to substantial refocussing of some of the argumentation. Edwin Ramage taught me what the real meaning of the word 'colleague' is, and without his help and encouragement I would never have completed this book. And finally there is Linda Waugh, whose own work impelled me to write a book I might not otherwise have written.

January 1981   R.B. Sangster
Bloomington, Indiana

The very essence of linguistics is the quest for meaning.
                                    Benjamin Lee Whorf (1936)

Only the correlations between signifier and signifier supply the standard for all research into meaning.
                                    Jacques Lacan (1957)

Perception should not be viewed as a grasping of external reality, but rather as the specification of one. Thus the external world [has] only a triggering role in the release of the internally-determined activity of the nervous system.
                                    Humberto Maturana (1980)

Introduction
Language as a System of Signs

The concept of sign has been central to the study of language since at least the time of the Stoics. Jakobson inherited the concept through the intermediary of Baudouin de Courtenay and Ferdinand de Saussure.[1] It is the principle of language as a system of signs that thoroughly unites the various theoretical postulates in this approach.

"The essential property of any sign in general, and of any linguistic sign in particular, is its twofold character."[2] The linguistic sign, at whatever level in language it may occur, is a bipartite entity consisting of a *signans* and a *signatum*. Saussure's elaboration of the nature of the linguistic sign was worked out primarily at the level of the morpheme, the smallest linguistic unit charged with its own meaning. Every morpheme is composed of a sound form – the *signifiant* or "image acoustique" in Saussure's terminology – associated with a meaning – the *signifié*. Saussure diagrammed this fundamental relationship in the following manner:[3]

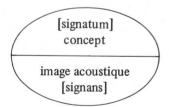

In Jakobson's formulation **all** linguistic units are signs: "every linguistic unit is bipartite and involves two aspects – one sensible and the other intelligible."[4] "Any linguistic, and in general semiotic, analysis resolves more complex units into smaller **but still semiotic** units."[5]

The phoneme is a semiotic unit, hence a sign, since it unites an invariant, recurring bundle of acoustic properties (signals) with a constant signification. Though the phoneme does not have a meaning of its own, it does signify "mere otherness": "the semiotic function of a phoneme within a higher linguistic unit is to denote that this unit has another meaning than an equipollent unit which *ceteris paribus* contains another phoneme in the same position."[6]

By the same reasoning the distinctive feature is also a sign. The definition of any phonological distinctive feature necessarily involves the isolation of an invariant set of physical properties – its *signans*;[7] and as the ultimate components of phonemes, distinctive features are the most elementary constituents that carry the capacity to distinguish meaning. As with the phoneme, therefore, the distinctive capacity of the feature is its *signatum*.

Likewise in syntactic analysis we have to do with signs. The study of word order, for example, can be treated in the same manner as that of phonology or morphology. The concept of linguistic sign implies that there exists a constant, recurring formal property or set of properties correlated with an invariant of meaning. A typical problem of word order would be, for example, the investigation of the change in *signata* brought about by the formal difference between pre-position and post-position of the adjective with respect to the noun in a given language. That such a syntactic problem is indeed a matter for semiotic analysis can be seen from the following diagram, which represents this particular syntactic property in terms of sign relationship.[8] This and other examples of syntactic phenomena are considered in Chapter 4 below.

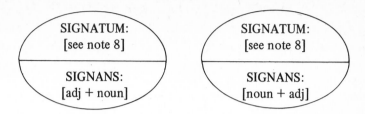

Thus the concept of sign basically involves a correlation between sound form and meaning. Stated in this manner, however, it is probably true that virtually all modern linguistic theories operate in some sense with the concept of sign, since all modern theories are ulimately concerned with the relationship between form and meaning in language. What distinguishes the present approach from other interpretations of this fundamental linguistic relationship is not so much a concern for the fact of the relationship itself as the particular understanding of the **nature** of the relationship.

As Jakobson has remarked, the "two constituents of any linguistic sign (and of any sign in general) necessarily **presuppose and require each other**."[9] This very strong and unequivocal position implies a direct and immediate relationship between form and meaning. "Speech sounds must be consistently analyzed with regard to meaning, and meaning, in its turn must be analyzed with reference to the sound form."[10] "An analysis of any linguistic sign whatever can be performed only on condition that its sensible aspect be examined in the light of its intelligible aspect (the *signans* in the light of the *signatum*) and vice versa."[11] From Jakobson's own statements as well as from a careful examination of his analysis of both sound and meaning in various languages, it is clear that, for him, there can be no *signans* without a *signatum*, and conversely, no *signatum* without a *signans*.[12]

This very special view of the nature of the linguistic sign was already explicit in Saussure. Jakobson actually derives from Saussure the notion that the meaningful properties of the sign are inseparable from its formal aspect. When Saussure defined language as a system of signs, each considered an "entité à deux faces," he meant quite literally that it is the sound form that carries the meaning directly. It was Saussure's conviction that "une entité matérielle n'existe que par le sens, la fonction dont elle est revêtue," and vice versa, that "un sens, une fonction n'existe que par le support de quelque forme matérielle."

In his recent review of the first two volumes of Jakobson's *Selected Writings*, Ladislav Matejka notes Jakobson's "recurrent emphasis on the indissoluble bond between the physical and mental aspects of verbal signs."[13] The inseparability of sound and meaning is, as Matejka points out, still very much a critical issue in Jakobson's thinking, something that he is at pains to emphasize even in his most recent writings. Such a view of the sound-meaning relationship is not only a cornerstone of his theory, but, I intend to show, a principle which, if applied rigorously, can give new direction to semantic investigation in the 1980's, just as it did to phonological research in the thirties and forties.

What is implied by the phrase "the inseparability of sound and meaning?" Clearly, the relationship between surface structure and semantic interpretation − between surface form and meaning − is not isomorphic in natural language. There is never a perfect one-to-one correlation between the formal and the semantic aspects of any language. What languages do present us with is a form-meaning relationship which is essentially asymmetrical. Now as linguists we have a choice: we can decide that this asymmetry implies a fundamental lack of correspondence between formal and semantic units in language, such that a separate set of abstract properties − deep structures − must be postulated to mediate between the two. Or we can conclude, with Jakobson, that such asymmetry does not imply a lack of solidarity between form and meaning, and that the essential operating principle of language remains one in which form and meaning directly support each other. In fact, this is the essence of the sign principle, that on the phonological level, sound forms (phonological oppositions) function primarily for the purpose of distinguishing meaning, and conversely, on the semantic level, "there is no conceptual opposition without a corresponding formal distinction."[14]

This latter view can have far-reaching consequences for semantic research. For one thing, such an interpretation suggests that, rather than assuming that the formal, surface data of language do not provide sufficient information for the construction of a semantic theory, we should instead consider the possibility that surface structures contain far more clues to semantic structure than we may be presently aware of. In fact, I shall argue that the most fruitful approach to semantic investigation is one where we actually adopt a principle of "formal determinism" for the purpose of extracting semantic invariance in natural language.

To argue successfully for such a position, however, some groundwork needs first to be laid. Specifically, in order to establish an adequate framework in which to present such an approach to semantic theory, we need first to consider the essential features of this approach as it has been applied to phonological description.

CHAPTER ONE

Phonology

1. THE SIGN PRINCIPLE AS APPLIED TO THE STRUCTURE OF SOUND

In 1958–1960, Jakobson wrote a most instructive article which places the concept of the linguistic sign in its historical perspective. "The Kazan' School of Polish Linguistics and its Place in the International Development of Phonology" traces the development of the application of the sign principle from the time of the Sanskrit and Greek theoreticians down to the modern interpretations of the first structuralists.[1] The article begins with the consideration of a set of related concepts that were established in Indian, Greek, and medieval thought. The Sanskrit grammarians, for example, invented the term *sphota* to designate "the sound form in respect to its semiotic value, which 'flows forth' from that form."[2] Thomas Aquinas operated with speech sounds as "'primarily designed to convey meaning' (*principialiter data ad significandum*)."[3] What each of these two views has in common in a concern with the immediate semiotic function of speech sounds, their necessary correlation with and capacity for distinguishing meanings. In Aquinas' case, Jakobson notes the primary concern with "the problem of the conversion of sounds into sign vehicles:"[4] "The main object of study is the way in which gross sound matter is processed and made usable for semiotic purposes."[5]

Equally revealing is the way in which Jakobson presents the work of Baudouin de Courtenay in this same article. The older Baudouin is specifically distinguished from the earlier, younger theoretician on the basis of his abandonment of a strictly functional (i.e., semiotic) approach to the study of sound in favor of a psychological approach. In presenting this fundamental change in Baudouin's thinking, Jakobson undeniably considers the development unfortunate and misguided, a return to the contemporary thinking from which Baudouin had earlier successfully managed to separate himself, much in the manner of Saussure. In Jakobson's words,

The place of functional investigations of speech sounds, investigations which the young Baudouin accented so strongly, was taken in his later lectures by something that he called 'psychophonetics'. The main object of his interest was no longer the relations between sound and meaning, but only the mental aspect of speech sounds.[6]

From this article we obtain an essential insight into what is meant by the autonomous, functional study of phonological entities: the nature of speech sounds cannot be properly investigated by studying their relationship to other, extra-linguistic phenomena, without having first determined the nature of speech sounds as *signantia*. And this more fundamental task can only be accomplished by investigating the intrinsically linguistic properties of sounds, that is, their capacity to distinguish meaning. "As phonemes are linguistic elements, it follows that no phoneme can be correctly defined except by linguistic criteria, i.e., by means of its function in the language."[7]

There is no doubt what Jakobson means by intrinsic linguistic properties. He quotes approvingly from Henry Sweet that "'language is essentially based on the dualism of form and meaning.' Hence all attempts to disregard this dualism and 'to reduce language to strict logical or psychological categories. . .have failed. . .'."[8] The association of sound with meaning is the primary linguistic relationship, the fundamental determinant of linguistic structure in a functional theory of language. Jakobson has constantly reiterated the strong need for applying intrinsically linguistic criteria to the treatment of verbal problems. "One must constantly remember that verbal processes and concepts — in short, all the *signantia* and *signata* in their interrelations —

require, first and foremost, a purely linguistic analysis and interpretation."[9] The concept of the linguistic sign makes it imperative that, when pursuing phonological analysis, "the sound shape of language cannot be exhaustively investigated without constant reference to meaning."[10]

It is important to note, however, that this position regarding the autonomous definition of sounds as sign vehicles in no way implies a denial of the existence of relationships between linguistic phenomena and other, related extra-linguistic phenomena — whether logical, psychological, physiological or whatever. Nor is there any denial of the urgent need to study such relationships. But there is very definitely implied here a theoretical and methodological priority: intrinsic properties must be determined before extrinsic relationships can be meaningfully investigated.

This is the lesson that Jakobson's research has repeatedly taught us.[11] What is being proposed is not an artificial separation of disciplines, but rather a RELATIVE AUTONOMY which is intended specifically to avoid the reductionist fallacies of much previous and some contemporary linguistic investigation. Moreover, the relative autonomy that Jakobson insists upon applies not only between disciplines, but necessarily operates also within the sphere of language itself. In the latter case it defines the nature of the hierarchical relationship among the various levels of linguistic phenomena such as phonology and grammar.

The concept of autonomy which is engendered by the functional, or semiotic, approach to phonological description has met with a good deal of criticism in the modern literature of phonology, much of it, unfortunately, the result of some fairly fundamental misunderstandings of what the concept is meant to imply. In the light of such misconceptions, therefore, it seems appropriate that we consider in greater detail the issue of autonomous phonemics, of how autonomy should be applied in phonological investigation.

2. THE PHONEME

Since so many American linguists have for some time now considered the concept of phonemics to be outmoded, it is important that we place this matter carefully in perspective. Jakobson
distinguishes three separate, but related, domains that pertain to
phonological entities: the phonemic, the morphophonemic,
and the system of distinctive features. The relationship between
the first two of these is especially crucial and will be the subject
of this section. The role of distinctive features is taken up in the
following two sections.

The phonemic and morphophonemic systems are viewed
as distinct, relatively autonomous domains in part because of
the different roles they play in speech perception and production
respectively. The system of phonemes is of primary importance
in the decoding of messages, whereas the system of morpho-
phonemes is essential in encoding. Moreover, the two functions
of encoding and decoding must not be confused.

The rules of verbal input and output are complementary and are not to be
mechanically intermingled. The phonemic cues are prior to the grammatical
unit for the listener, whereas the phonemic operations of the speaker are
grammatical prerequisites: the two opposite linguistic views of the hierarchical order between morphophonemics and phonemics proper simply
mirror two different frames of reference, namely the standpoints of the
two participants in the speech event.[12]

The making of autonomous phonemic discriminations is an
indispensable component of the decoding process, prior to and
separate from the application of any grammatical information at
this stage of the speech event. "The perceiver is bound to begin
his decoding by using the physical properties of the sound. . .;
the very token must first be converted into a sign-vehicle before
any grammatical. . .procedures can be operative."[13] And in fact,
"the number of strictly autonomous decisions which are required
for the identification of phonemes in an utterance and cannot
be deduced from any grammatical rules remains very sizable."[14]
Morphophonemic patterning, on the other hand, which is cen-

tral to the encoding process, necessarily involves grammatical prerequisites.

Nowhere is the distinction between phonemic and morphophonemic processes more apparent than in the resolution of ambiguity in language. The rules of patterning in the morphophonemic system present all ambiguities as ultimately resolvable at the grammatical level, which represents the point of view of the speaker. For the addressee, on the other hand, no amount of grammatical information will suffice to resolve an ambiguity, since in the process of perception all possible grammatical structures are equally probable. The hearer has no other recourse than to turn to the verbal or non-verbal environment to find the necessary cues for disambiguation, if there are any. And it is precisely this latter operation that is embodied in the concept of the phoneme in the traditional sense. In this context Jakobson has noted the following:

Again and again, we must insist on the perceiver's probabilistic attitude toward the verbal input; he cannot do without phonemic discrimination, and to break the homonyms he looks for cues in the heteronymous and unisensical context. For the encoder, homonymy is naturally devoid of any ambiguity, whereas the decoder may find no cue to decipher a homonym even in its verbal environment.[15]

In support of the position that the phonemic and morphophonemic systems represent two relatively autonomous domains, Jakobson has adduced a broad range of evidence from neurophysiological studies and observations on the processes of language acquisition. He has noted, for example, that:

The substantial difference between the encoding and decoding operations in verbal behaviour is eloquently documented by the typology of aphasic disorders, and namely by the striking dissimilarity between the so-called motor, predominantly encoding, and the so-called sensory, primarily decoding, impairments. It is particularly significant that the latter type of aphasia, in contradistinction to the former, is characterized by the loss of those syntactical, morphological, lexical, and phonemic elements which are not determined by the context. In particular, the less some components of a phoneme are dependent on their simultaneous and sequential environment, the sooner they are subject to deletion. The disturbances in phoneme-finding lay bare the strictly discriminatory selective operation as the immediate aim of the decoding process.[16]

Likewise, with regard to first- and second-language learning, we are reminded that:

A passive acquisition of foreign languages usually precedes their contingent active mastery. Russians in the Caucasus often learn to understand one of the local languages and to discern by ear its 60 or 70 consonants without being able to reproduce them or even grasp the articulatory model of such frequent Caucasian phonemes as the glottalized stops. [. . .] Opposite cases of foreign phonemes reproduced in pronunciation but confused in perception are most exceptional.

Many studies of children's language have disclosed that words which were clearly distinguished in their perceptual experience and memory remained homonymous in their own utterances so long as the phonemic distinctions involved were familiar to the child only on the sensory but not yet on the motor level. [. . .] The foreigners and children cited have stored in their memory an adequate table of phonemes and of their sensory actualizations without having grasped the corresponding vocal-tract configurations.[17]

These observations demonstrate that the phonemic and morphophonemic processes in language are in fact irreducible to each other, and that a separate set of phonemic operations is both justified and necessary in linguistic description. The phoneme, therefore, cannot be considered an artificial construct. In fact, to dispense with a separate phonemic level and construct a model of language which is supposed to represent the linguistic competence of an "ideal speaker-hearer" does indeed make a scholastic fiction out of language.

Because speech production and perception do represent relatively autonomous domains of linguistic structure, it is quite improper to use arguments appropriate in one domain to invalidate concepts in the other. Such a mode of argumentation has been implicit in attacks on the validity of the phoneme beginning with Halle's initial line of reasoning in the *Sound Pattern of Russian* (1959). The primary rationale behind these attacks is that a separate level of phonemic representation is not justified because in some instances maintaining such an independent level makes it impossible to state certain linguistically significant generalizations in their simplest form. Halle's original argument was made with respect to voicing assimilation in obstruent clusters in Russian. Because voicing is distinctive (phonemic) in all Russian obstruents except /č/, /c/, and /x/, the process of assimilation produces different phonemes in all but these three cases, where the alternation remains phonetic (allophonic). From the point of view of speech production, there is obviously a single assimilatory process at work here, despite the fact that the voicing is phonemic in some segments and sub-phonemic in others. As true as this observation may be, however, it in no way affects the actual phonemic status of voicing in Russian which, from the point of view of the addressee, produces a clear distinction between the three obstruents /č/, /c/, and /x/ on the one hand, and all other obstruents on the other.

A more appropriate way of viewing the facts in such situations would be to realize that the type of information codified at the phonemic level is paradigmatic, whereas at the phonetic level the information present is primarily syntagmatic. And each of these two distinct types of information is crucial to the functioning of language. In the three Russian obstruents /č/, /c/, and /x/, the feature of voicing has no paradigmatic function anywhere in the language (i.e., it cannot be used to distinguish words of different meaning); it does, however, have a syntagmatic function, producing voiced allophones in the context of a following voiced obstruent. In all other obstruents in Russian, voicing carries both a syntagmatic and a paradigmatic function: it functions both in the assimilatory process in obstruent clusters and elsewhere as a means of distinguishing words of different meaning. Furthermore, there is no dearth of experimental evidence to show that the paradigmatic function is just as psychologically "real" as the syntagmatic one. As Bruce Derwing has noted,

in word initial position, for example, the voiced-voiceless pairs (such as *t-d*, *s-z*, etc.) are readily distinguished by all Russian speakers... Difficulties crop up, however, in distinguishing such pairs as *c-ʒ*, *č-ǯ*, *x-ɣ* in obstruent clusters, where ... the members of each pair are merely predictable variants of a single underlying distinctive element.[18]

And as Charles Ferguson remarked in his discussion of Halle's voicing rule for Russian, the situation is quite parallel to the devoicing of final consonants in Turkish, which is sometimes phonemic and sometimes phonetic:

We must note that the devoicing of final stops and affricates is functionally different from the devoicing of final /r, l/. When a Turk hears a new word (e.g., a proper name or a new technical term) ending in a voiceless stop or affricate, he does not know how to treat that word morphophonemically, i.e., whether the consonant in question may be voiced elsewhere in the paradigm.[19]

This is because the Turkish speaker "knows" there is additional paradigmatic information present in the case of stops and affricates that is not present in the liquids.

Actually, there should be no argument here at all, for it is quite evident that the autonomy of phonemics does not appear in its optimal form in speech production, but rather only in speech perception, where purely phonemic discriminations take precedence over grammatical prerequisites in the directional chain sound ⟶ meaning. It is this **ascendent** operation that reveals the autonomous character of the phonemic level, whereas the **descendent** operation (from meaning to sound) is what underlies the development of morphophonemics.[20] In the latter operation there is no clear-cut division between levels, and consequently phonological alternations frequently involve both phonemic and sub-phonemic alternants at the same time. It is the attempt to define both levels on the descendent operation alone which creates the confusion and makes it appear that separate levels are unjustified.

The reductionism inherent in this kind of argument against the phoneme sets a dangerous precedent for linguistic analysis. Phonemics and morphophonemics represent two **relatively** autonomous domains of linguistic structure, both grounded in the same set of primitive elements (the distinctive features), yet each having different principles of organization. The distinctiveness of the two disciplines is just as evident as their obvious interdependence, and neither aspect can be ignored at the expense of the other. It is the very essence of relative autonomy that two hierarchically different levels should be distinct without being totally independent of one another. As Jakobson has put it, "The grammatical and phonemic structures mutually readjust each other. The relative internal autonomy of both patterns does not exclude their perpetual interaction and interdependence, [for] neither does the autonomy of these two linguistic aspects mean independence, nor does their co-ordinate interdependence imply a lack of autonomy."[21] Just as we must avoid the kind of strict separation of levels which refuses to admit of interplay between the various hierarchical modes of a unified linguistic structure, so too must we guard against the opposite fallacy, which "forcibly subjects one level to another's rules and denies the former's own patterning as well as its self generating development."[22]

I will return in the next chapter to a more thorough discussion of the nature of morphophonemics. For the moment there still remain to be considered certain technical difficulties which appear to be unresolvable when operating at the level of the traditional phoneme, and these will be taken up at this time. These difficulties have been pointed out on numerous occasions, starting as early as Bernard Bloch's well-known article on "Phonemic Overlapping" in 1941, and more recently catalogued by Chomsky in the chapter on autonomous phonemics in his *Current Issues in Linguistic Theory* of 1964. All of the issues raised in these discussions of the inadequacies inherent in the phoneme concept, however, seem unresolvable only if one operates with the phoneme as an indivisible unit, a phonological minimum, which it is not. One must understand that phonemes are not the ultimate phonological constituents of language, but are further analyzable into distinctive features. It is within the system of distinctive features that the ultimate differential components of the verbal sign are found, and it is there that we must look for the solution to problems in phonemics.

3. INVARIANCE AT THE LEVEL OF DISTINCTIVE FEATURES

In order to understand how difficulties that seem inherent in the traditional phoneme are resolvable at the level of distinctive features, the concept of invariance itself must be carefully scrutinized.

The linguist's analysis of sound into a discrete set of distinctive features recapitulates the process by which languages select from gross sound matter a relatively small number of invariant oppositions which function to distinguish meaning. In describing the nature of such oppositions, however, it would be a serious theoretical and methodological error to assume that what is opposed is a set of constant and absolute physical properties. Rather, all such oppositions must be defined in RELATIONAL terms, for "any distinctive feature exists only 'as a term of relation'. The definition of such a phonemic invariant cannot be made in absolute terms — it cannot refer to a metric resemblance but must be based solely on relational equivalence."[23] The invariant associated with any distinctive phonological opposition is in fact a TOPOLOGICAL invariant: it is an abstract, relational quality that remains constant through the various transformations it undergoes as a result of its occurrence in concrete contexts. These two characteristics, relativity and topology, define the essence of phonological oppositions and, we might add, find their analogues in the definition of semantic oppositions as well.[24]

Jakobson has adduced innumerable examples to demonstrate the relational and topological nature of phonemic oppositions and the manner in which distinctive features are combined contextually into bundles, or phonemes. One such example concerns the French phonemic pattern.

In the system of French consonants the feature of compactness presents three contextual variants, each of which depends on a concurrent feature: compact consonants are implemented as velar when plosive, as palatal when nasal, and as postalveolar when continuant. In terms of speech synthesis, the transformation of French compact consonants from stops into nasals or fricatives converts the velar region of articulation into palatal or postalveolar respectively, **while their relative compactness remains invariant [. . .]**

The localization difference between the French stops and the corresponding continuants is an appropriate warning against the oversimplified view of a phoneme as a mechanical aggregate of materially invariable components. Every combination of distinctive features into simultaneous bundles results in a specific contextual variation.[25]

And again, with respect to the Bulgarian vowel pattern:

Each of the three tonality classes — acute (front), grave flat (back rounded), and grave non-flat (back unrounded) — is represented by a pair compact (wider) — diffuse (narrower) — namely, /e/ – /i/, /o/ –/u/, /a/ – /ə/. The physico-motor propinquity between /ə/, the diffuse phoneme of the last pair, and the compact phonemes of the other two pairs, /e/ and /o/, has no phonemic pertinence, for the same opposition underlies all three pairs: /a/ is to /ə/ as /e/ is to /i/ as /o/ is to /u/.

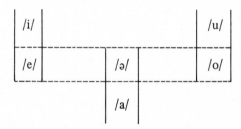

The wider articulation of /a/ and /ə/ as compared to both other pairs is a contextual variation associated with the concurrence of grave and non-flat (velarity with unroundness); but **the purely abstract topological relations remain unchanged** in all three pairs. Here we are dealing with phenomenal forms whose specific properties are. . .'disponible': such properties are not affected by a modification of the absolute data upon which they rest.[26]

Instances of so-called "phonemic overlapping" illustrate particularly well the relational and topological nature of phonological invariants at the feature level. In such cases, what are the same phonetic characteristics when measured in absolute terms appear to implement more than one phoneme in different environments. The appearance of overlapping, however, is itself created by the methodologically improper procedure of measuring only the sounds' absolute phonetic value, i.e., of "measur[ing] the sound matter without reference to the rule of dichotomy imposed upon it by language."[27] As soon as the ultimate phonemic constituents, the distinctive features, are properly viewed as terms of binary oppositions, and the appropriate relational measurements of the sound matter are made, no overlapping results. The problem is parallel to the situation common in music where, for example, F-flat and E have one and the same absolute acoustic value, but represent two different musical values, as the following example illustrates.

As music imposes upon sound matter a graduated scale, similarly language imposes upon it the dichotomous scale which is simply a corollary of the purely differential role played by phonemic entities. [. . .] In different positions the relation strong/weak can be implemented by different variants: for instance, in a strong (stressed, initial, etc.) position, by an aspirated, fortis stop vs. a lenis stop (voiced or unvoiced), and in a weak position by matching two non-aspirated stops – a fortis and a lenis one, or two spirants – an unvoiced and a voiced one. In Danish this opposition strong/weak is implemented by *t* vs. *d* in strong position, and by *d* vs. *đ* in weak position, so that the weak phoneme in the strong position **materially** coincides with the strong phoneme in the weak position. The relation strong/weak in any position is perfectly measurable both physically and physiologically, as in general every phonemic opposition presents, in all its manifestations, a common denominator both on the acoustic and the articulatory level. But if one should measure the sound matter without reference to the rule of dichotomy imposed upon it by language, the conclusion would be that there are 'overlapping' phonemes, in the same way as a physicist with his acoustic instruments. . .fails to explain why, in a given piece of music, F-flat and E represent two different values.[28]

Because any distinctive feature is a topological invariant, it may be implemented by a range of phonetic variation determined by the context – both the concurrent and sequential environment – in which it occurs. Thus, "the concurrent and sequential bits of information implemented in an utterance stand in a one-to-one relation with the distinctive features."[29] The isomorphic relationship is always in force, for it is the defining characteristic of any truly differential element. "On the level of features every distinctive opposition is endowed with a perceptual constancy: and as far as the features are properly defined in purely relational terms, no overlapping can arise. The relational invariant of each oppositional pair is **per definitionem** actualized in every context where the given feature occurs, unless this feature is omitted in an elliptical variety of speech."[30]

It is important to remember when applying these principles that one must operate with the optimal, explicit code of a language, and not with an elliptical or otherwise reduced sub-code, or mixture of codes. So many of the examples adduced in criticism of so-called taxonomic phonemics fail to appreciate the fact that elliptical and other derivative varieties of speech are themselves transforms of a more explicit code, and as such are regularly deducible from the latter. The distinctive features for a given language must themselves be defined on the most explicit, optimal code, or "full style" of speech. Failure to do this leads to such unwarranted conclusions as, for example, the contention that the pronunciation of inter-vocalic /t/ and /d/ in American English violates the principle of phonemic invariance in such pairs as 'writer' − 'rider' and 'latter' − 'ladder'. In fact, the distinctive difference relevant in such pairs, that of tenseness vs. laxness in the medial consonant, is fully recoverable in the explicit code of English where "the most stable cue to the distinction of tense and lax phonemes remains the greater duration of the former."[31] That another feature, whether itself distinctive or redundant, should assume the function of tenseness in the rapid variety of speech − as vowel length in the preceding syllable does in the present example − is a perfectly normal process, one that is typical of transformations from an optimal code to another variety of speech.

4. THE FUNCTIONS OF THE DISTINCTIVE FEATURES

Since the distinctive features are the ultimate constituents of any phonological system, they necessarily play a fundamental role in both speech perception and production. "Both on the motor and on the sensory level every distinctive feature is plainly readable and displays the same polarity and invariance when viewed in rigorously relational terms,. . .[for] 'articulation and sound waves never go separate ways'."[32] In their phonemic or "sense-discriminating" role features serve as a relatively autonomous phonological decoding device, whereas in their morphophonemic or "sense-determining" role they act primarily as a morphological (or better: morpheme-structuring) device, serving to differentiate and classify the various grammatical processes.[33] An adequate linguistic theory must account for both of these crucial functions, but it must do so with the clear understanding that it is the distinctive features and not the phoneme that carry this dual function. The confusion on this point is, in my opinion, the factor most responsible for the split in modern linguistics between structuralism and generative phonology. And the continuing misunderstanding of the issues involved here is also, I believe, what prevents many linguists from reembracing the structuralist point of view as they look for ways out of the impasse created by the abstractness controversy in generative grammar. To illustrate this point, let us return once more to the place where the controversy over autonomous phonemics began: to Halle's example of voicing assimilation in obstruent clusters in a language like Russian.

As we noted above (page 15), the process of assimilation in this case involves an alternation where the feature of voicing is neutralized. Sometimes the alternating segments are positional variants of one and the same phoneme, in which case we have to do with allophonic variation, and other times the process involves the neutralization of the voicing opposition between two different phonemes − that is, the type of positional restriction that the now obsolete term 'archiphoneme' was originally intended to cover. The reason why the term 'archiphoneme' is outmoded is of particular importance to this discussion, for the use of this term in Prague School theory corresponds to the time when the solution to problems presented by alternations was still being sought at the phoneme level. As we have since learned, problems involving alternations find their resolution not in terms of phonemes, whose function is properly viewed as discriminatory, but rather in terms of distinctive features, which relate to both sense discrimination and determination. In any phonological alternation we have to do with the neutralization of feature oppositions, and whether the features involved are distinctive **in a particular segment** or not is of no consequence in the functioning of alternations. Sometimes, in fact, there will be no way to determine unequivocally what phoneme underlies a given alternating series of phonemes, but this is only because phonemes don't underlie phonemes; features do. Since the distinctive features are the invariants that operate in both the descendent and ascendent aspects of language (i.e., for the speaker as well as the hearer), this means that there never will be a case where an alternation neutralizes a feature that does not have a distinctive (i.e., phonemic) function somewhere else in the language in question. Hence all phonological alternations will be statable in terms of the same set of features that describes the set of phonemes in a language. And the problem of assigning the alternating segments in question to one or another phoneme consequently becomes entirely moot.

The lesson to be drawn from these observations is that neither the set of phonemes in a given language nor the system of rules that describes the alternations that occur, taken in isolation the one from the other, can possibly represent the competence of an ideal speaker-hearer. It is only at the level of the distinctive features that the two functions come together in a single, unifying structure; and this very fact provides the most natural solution possible to the problem of how abstract are phonological entities. The features that possess this dual function are just those that are distinctive in the technical sense of the term – that is, those that display paradigmatic as well as syntagmatic distributional properties. This fact is evident from the distribution of alternating segments. Of two alternating sounds, only one will occur in a restricted environment (i.e., will be syntagmatically conditioned). The other will appear in a position where either of the two could occur – that is, in a position of potential contrastive distribution. Thus alternations directly reflect the paradigmatic properties that are inherent in the dintinctive features, and this is what makes the selection of so-called base forms a non-arbitrary process. The presence of independent paradigmatic function is what distinguishes sound qualities that are **distinctive** from those that are merely **distinct** in a particular synchronic state of a language. The latter — which include such features as tenseness and gravity in the Russian vowel system, or aspiration in English consonants — display only syntagmatic distributional properties, and are therefore properly termed REDUNDANT features. For the most part these features des- cribe allophones, whose distribution is entirely complementary — that is, unlike alternations, **all** the variants described by redun- dant features occur in restricted environments. The primary function of these features is to act as support for the distinctive features. Since redundant features are in a strictly dependent re- lation to the distinctive features, they cannot enter independently into paradigmatic oppositions. They may, and frequently do, replace distinctive features under specific conditions, in which case they may assume a distinctive function, but the distinctive oppositions whose place they take are always unambiguously recoverable. The rules that account for this process of replace- ment and the conditions under which it occurs are an indispen- sable part of phonological description, but they must not be confused with (or mechanically intermingled with) the rules that govern alternations. The functional difference between the two is clearly evident in the data of non-elliptic speech — that is, in the so-called full style that underlies all varieties of speech, where the different distributional properties noted above are readily observable. The occurrence of redundant features in positions of distinctive opposition are properly accounted for by the set of rules that relates elliptic and other marked varieties of speech to the underlying full style, thus maintaining the functional dichotomy of feature types as well as the relative autonomy of the various styles of speech. As far as I am aware, such a set of rules has never been elaborated, at least not within the present framework, and this remains an urgent task. We need to know how these rules differ from those that govern alternations so that we can better appreciate the interplay between sound qualities that are distinctive and those that are merely distinct. There is already abundant evidence for the weaker discriminatory power of the latter as compared with the former, and the fundamental differences in distributional properties between the two are beyond question, but the nature of the processes — both diachronic and synchronic — that relate the two requires extensive investigation.

Returning our attention to those features that are distinctive, we should note that one of the two functions they fulfill clearly takes precedence over the other. As the very term distinctive implies, it is the phonemic function that predominates:

The obviously primary function, the sense-discriminative (purely distinctive) one, assigns to the feature the capability of signaling — with a probability near to 1.0 — the semantic likeness or nonlikeness of two meaningful verbal units. The second task, which necessarily presupposes the first, is a sense-determinative or, in the terminology launched by the Prague Circle, 'morphophonological' function; the arrangement of features supplies information about the derivational and/or flexional structure and grammatical meaning of the units in question.[34]

The reason that the distinctiveness of a feature is its primary characteristic is simply because, in the final analysis, all linguistic elements are signs. Since all the formal devices of language serve ultimately as a means of communication, it follows that when analyzing the ultimate constituents of the sound system of a language, we consider first how they fulfill their sign function. This implies in turn that the identification of acoustic cues be given preference over the determination of motor correlates in the description of any feature. Since this, too, is a subject of some contention in current phonological theory, let us look more closely at the reasoning involved.

In what sense does the sign function determine the priority of acoustic over articulatory cues in the establishment of distinctive features? The answer to this question lies in the very concept of a functional model of language. In such a model, language is viewed as purposeful human behavior, as goal-directed activity; and the primary objective of linguistic science is "to analyze all the instrumentalities of language from the standpoint of the tasks they perform."[35] Our approach is essentially a teleological one where language is seen as a tool for communication, a semiotic instrument.[36] In phonological analysis, "the teleological conception of sound problems increases the relevance of acoustical analysis in comparison with the physiology of speech,. . .since [it is] not the motor but the acoustical aspect of speech sounds, aimed at by the speaker, [which] has a social value."[37]

Since the motor stage of any speech event is to the acoustical phenomenon as the means to its effect, the relations on the acoustical level seem to give a more efficient key to the generative invariances in relationship than vice versa. Any feature displays a much more conspicious opposition of its alternatives on the acoustical level than on the motor level, so that a listing of distinctive features in terms of their articulatory correlates without any acoustical correspondents inevitably remains an imprecise and inconclusive torso.[38]

If we consider for a moment the historical antecedents of this approach, it is worth noting that Saussure already realized the necessity for looking to the acoustic data for the primary cues to the ultimate nature of speech sounds. In his sketches for a major treatise on phonetics, Saussure consistently viewed speech production as "programmed, intentional, anticipatory activity. . . The 'present', namely the *phonème en exécution* is guided by the 'future': *le phonème à exécuter, l'idée du phonème qui en suit est ce qui dirige l'articulation.*"[39] "*En revanche l'ensemble du fait physiologique est exclusivement connu dans sa relation avec le fait acoustique.*"[40]

The development of distinctive feature theory within the framework of a functional approach to language has proceeded since the time of Saussure with the clear conviction that antecedent stages of the speech event must be defined in terms of subsequent stages and not the other way around. In the *Thèses* presented by the members of the Prague Linguistic Circle to the

Premier Congrès des Philologues Slaves in 1929, it is stated un-equivocally that:

Le problème du finalisme des phénomènes phonologiques fait que, dans l'étude du côté extérieur de ces phénomènes, c'est l'analyse acoustique qui doit ressortir au premier plan, car c'est précisément l'image acoustique et non l'image motrice qui est visée par le sujet parlant.[41]

The publication of the *Fundamentals of Language* shows that this was the guiding principle in the elaboration of the distinctive feature concept in the years leading up to the 1950's.

The closer we are in our investigation to the destination of the message, the more accurately we can gauge the information conveyed by the sound chain. . . This determines the operational hierarchy of levels in their decreasing pertinence: perceptual, aural, acoustical, motor (the latter carry-ing no direct information to the receiver except for the sporadic help of lip reading). . . In the process of communication there is no single-value infer-ence from a succeeding to a preceding stage. With each successive stage the selectivity increases; some data of an antecedent stage are irrelevant for any subsequent stage and each item of the latter stage may be a function of several variables from the former stage. . . The specification of distinctive oppositions may be made with respect to any stage of the speech event, from articulation to perception and decoding, on the sole condition that the invariants of any antecedent stage be selected and correlated in terms of the subsequent stages, given the evident fact that we speak to be heard, and need to be heard in order to understood.[42]

That this remains today the primary orientation of the function-al approach is evident from Jakobson's most recent writings, especially *The Sound Shape of Language*.[43]

The most meaningful illustrations of this principle can be found in those instances where there occurs a many-to-one re-lationship between the articulatory and the acoustic correlates for a given feature. Such instances are frequently used as evi-dence that phonological features should be defined in articulatory **rather than** acoustic terms. In such cases, it is argued, maintain-ing the primacy of acoustic criteria artificially limits the number of distinctive features, making it impossible to account for the true articulatory variety of feature types. Jakobson has responded to one of the more frequently cited examples of just this sort of relationship in a study examining the variety of consonantal articulations in African and Caucasian languages.[44] Of the three varieties of extrapulmonic consonants — ejective, implosives, and clicks — none ever participates in an autonomous phonemic opposition with respect to either of the others in a given language. For this reason separate features to describe them are simply not justified; rather, all three are "to be treated as different implementations of one and the same distinctive feature: checked — unchecked."[45] So long as the articulatory varieties observed share an acoustic identity and participate in a single phonemic opposition, no proliferation of features is required.

In the final analysis, however, we must again insist that we are not concerned with substituting an acoustic classification for an articulatory one but solely with uncovering the most productive criterion of division valid for both aspects.[46] For any distinctive feature we can determine, and must state, both its articulatory and its acoustic correlates. That the latter, the acoustic, relationships prove to be the ones which allow for the greater degree of generality in determining feature types, only serves to support the hypothesis that the semiotic function of distinctive features is their most important (defining) characteristic. It is, of course, true that the acoustic cues correspond more directly to the decoding, or phonemic, aspect of language, but this in no way limits their relevance for describing the processes involved in speech production. Ultimately both processes can be explained by a single set of features, so long as the features themselves are describable in both articulatory and acoustic terms.

It is the mechanism of speech production and the study of the distinctive features in their sense-determining role that we now turn our attention. The following chapter examines the nature of morphophonological and phonological processes that constitute the sense-determining function of the distinctive features.

CHAPTER TWO

Morphophonemics

1. DEFINITION AND SCOPE OF THE SUBJECT

As we saw in the preceding chapter, phonemics and morphophonemics represent two relatively autonomous domains of linguistic structure which are related to one another not, as has been frequently assumed, in a hierarchical fashion where the latter is taken to be simply a higher level with more abstract units than the former, but rather as two parallel domains with largely separate functions which are related through the intermediary of the distinctive features. In this chapter I want to describe precisely what processes are involved in morphophonemics, and will therefore be recasting the term in a more specific, technical framework than it appeared in the preceding chapter, where it was used to refer somewhat loosely to the range of phenomena associated with sense determination. As before, I find that the principles have been most elegantly formulated by Jakobson, and consequently I will follow his reasoning fairly closely.

In Jakobson's formulation, morphophonemics is technically **the study of phonemic patterning in morphology** – that is, of the "form structure of word grammar."[1] By this definition morphophonemics clearly belongs more to the discipline of morphology than to phonology, and it is the consequences of this fact that will occupy our attention in this chapter. Consistent with the application of linguistic sign theory, the study of "form structure" in morphology constitutes part of a larger discipline, the other half of which involves the "structure of meaning". Jakobson frequently utilizes terminology originally suggested by Sapir in referring to these two sub-disciplines of morphology, and speaks of 'processes' and 'concepts'.[2] The term 'concepts' concerns those semantically relevant categories for which there is formal expression in a given language, while 'processes' denotes the actual means of expression themselves.

The process of the inquiry into the sense-determinative function of the distinctive features promises an ever deeper analysis of subjects such as the makeup of morphemes, their selection and combinations, so that morphology will evolve into a phonological description of 'grammatical processes' indissolubly connected with the semantic scrutiny of corresponding 'grammatical concepts'.[3]

Morphophonemics, then, is "that part of morphology which is concerned with processes."[4]

As we progress from a mere catalogue of the grammatical meanings which occur in a given language to an analysis of their arrangements and mutual connections, we must pay still greater attention to the phonemic composition of the diverse formal units and especially to the repertories of phonemes and phonemic clusters specific for the single classes of those units.. . . The study of a grammatical pattern inevitably leads up to the problem of the phonemic means utilized for the expression of the diverse grammatical categories of the given language.. . . As soon as word grammar proceeds. . . from the 'structure of meaning' to the 'form structure', we find ourselves in the domains of morphophonemics, because a purely formal analysis of paradigms means nothing other than the disclosure of the phonemic similarity and distinctness of different paradigms, their members and components.[5]

It is important to realize that this conceptualization of morphophonemics is much broader than the mere study of alternations, though certain types of alternations remain an essential component of morphophonemics. All formal aspects of morphology, whether paradigmatic or syntagmatic, are included within the scope of this definition. In Jakobson's words,

That part of morphology which is concerned with processes must investigate the phonemic composition of morphemes and the formal differences between the grammatical classes of morphemes and words, namely differeı.ɔes in number, order, and selective set of phonemes and features. With the gradual improvement of linguistic analysis, paradigms change from mere catalogues into coherent systems of structured convergences and divergences. In accordance with this development, the difference between the traditional *Formenlehre* and the so-called morphophonemics vanishes, and the former actually turns into the latter. This merger became imminent as soon as the earlier exclusive preoccupation of morphophonemics with the phonemic alternations within identical morphemes was supplemented with an inquiry into phonemic syncretisms and dissimilarities within total classes of morphemes.[6]

We can illustrate how this approach is applied to the study of specific morphological categories by considering Jakobson's analysis of the grammatical morphology of the Russian verb. Though presented in several parts over a span of some 25 years, this analysis should be viewed as an intergrated whole, each of the parts of which gains in significance when considered in relation to the others. Three articles are involved: "Zur Struktur des russischen Verbums," written in 1931 and published in the following year; "Russian Conjugation," composed and published in 1948; and "Shifters, Verbal Categories, and the Russian Verb," prepared in 1956.[7]

The last of these three studies (Shifters) presents a synthesis of the entire subject, dividing the material into two major subdivisions, grammatical concepts on the one hand and grammatical processes on the other. Under the first heading is included an analysis of all the semantic categories for which there is formal expression in the Russian verbal grammatical system: person, gender, number, tense, aspect, mood, voice, and taxis. This section recapitulates (with certain modifications) the essence of what was originally presented in the 1931 study, which was devoted entirely to the analysis of grammatical concepts in the Russian verb. The second section of the Shifters article elaborates upon the different types of formal elements that are used to express the various conceptual categories previously established, substantiating the observation that different conceptual categories tend to make use of different grammatical processes. Included in this section is a presentation of the underlying formal shape of Russian verbal morphemes, with reference to the 1948 study for specific details. This latter study, "Russian Conjugation," is in its turn concerned primarily with the problem of alternations in Russian verbal inflection and with establishing a single underlying form for each simple verb stem in the language.

Inclusion of this latter analysis within the confines of a total description of Russian verbal morphology is particularly significant. For one thing, one cannot overlook the fact that "Russian Conjugation" is purposefully included by Jakobson in his *Selected Writings* under the heading "Morphological Studies", despite the fact that this particular article has for some time been at the center of discussions — primarily among American linguists — on the scope of **phonological** analysis. Clearly, there is a difference in focus here, the implications of which are, I believe, substantial. The analysis of those phonological alternations which constitute the core of the formal structure of the Russian verbal system are considered part and parcel of the larger study of the totality of the grammatical processes involved in Russian verbal morphology. As such they are distinct from other alternations in the language which do not function as a structuring device of the verbal system.

2. THE STRUCTURE AND FUNCTIONS OF ALTERNATIONS

The emphasis here on defining and classifying alternations according to their principal function in a language is a crucial feature of the present approach. From this point of view, the essence of an alternation is determined by its synchronic function in a given language: if an alternation functions primarily as a structural device (formal indicator) for a particular grammatical category or categories, then it is a true morphophonemic alternation. If, on the other hand, an alternation is not associated with any particular grammatical category, then we are dealing with a purely phonological alternation. With this functional approach, then, we have a principled basis for distinguishing between the two disciplines of morphophonemics and phonology proper, and can place the former in its proper perspective vis-à-vis the discipline of morphology, without making any artificial claims of autonomy.[8]

To substantiate this view, let us look further into the nature of alternations. If we were to construct a typology of alternations strictly in accordance with their synchronic function in a particular language, we would have to observe the following. What distinguishes a morphophonemic alternation from a purely phonological one is the fact that there are always morphological conditioning factors present in the former which are absent in the latter. There may also be phonological conditioning present as well in a morphophonemic alternation, but the presence of such additional conditioning must not be construed as representing the essence of the alternation, which remains morphological. A purely phonological alternation, on the other hand, contains no morphological conditioning; i.e., such an alternation occurs irrespective of grammatical categories, and therefore may be termed **automatic**.[9]

It is important to realize that in classifying alternations in terms of conditioning factors, we are concerned with the influence of both the sequential and the concurrent environment of the alternation in question.[10] In other words, both syntagmatic and paradigmatic factors are crucial for defining the essence of an alternation. Let us consider some examples. In Russian there is a phonological rule that only palatalized and palatal consonants can occur before the vowel /e/, except in unassimilated foreign words. This rule operates everywhere in the language irrespective of grammatical category. It is therefore an automatic alternation, where the sole conditioning factor is the sequential phonological environment. Likewise, voicing assimilation in Russian obstruent clusters (described above) is an example of the same type.

On the other hand, an alternation such as *a* ~ *an* in English is not automatic, although there is phonological conditioning present. Which alternant occurs depends upon whether the first segment of the following word is a vowel or a consonant, but outside the morphological category of indefinite article the same sequential conditioning factors do not produce the alternation. What makes this alternation qualitatively different from the preceding type is the additional presence of paradigmatic, morphological conditioning. In other words, this alternation contains additional morphological information that is not present in the other type, namely information concerning membership in a particular grammatical category. When we look at an alternation in terms of its function as a vehicle for conveying information, then the qualitative difference between phonemic and morphophonemic devices immediately asserts itself. The information that is conveyed morphophonemically may be highly limited – i.e., a morphophonemic alternation may signal nothing more than membership in a particular grammmatical category – , but that is already substantively different from the nature of information signalled phonologically, which concerns only the type of sound.

Most genuine morphophonemic alternations are both phonologically and morphologically conditioned at the same time. For example, the choice between the desinences *–ov* and *–ej* in the genitive plural of Russian nouns is completely determined by the nature of the preceding (stem final) consonant: if the consonant is palatalized or a husher (*š, ž, č,* or *šč*), *–ej* occurs, otherwise *–ov*. But elsewhere, outside the category of genitive plural, no such alternation takes place. Likewise, in Russian, consonant mutations – especially the velar ~ palatal alternations – are widespread, occurring rather systematically in certain verbal categories and somewhat more restrictedly in nominal derivation. For the most part these alternations are phonologically conditioned in that the distribution of the alternants can be described in many cases in terms of the nature of the following vocalic segment; but consonant mutation is not automatic in Russian because outside of the specified morphological categories, identical phonological conditions do not produce the alternations. In nominal derivation, for example, /k/ > /č/, /g/ > /ž/ is quite systematic before front vowels: *ruká ~ ručišča, reká ~ réčen'ka, kníga ~ knížica,* etc.; but in nominal inflection the alternation does not take place: *kníga* 'nom. sg.' vs. *knígi* 'gen. sg./nom. pl.' or *kníge* 'loc. sg.', *reká* 'nom. sg.' vs. *rekí* 'gen. sg.' or *réki* 'nom. pl.' or *reké* 'loc. sg.'.

Finally, there are alternations where only morphological conditioning is present. For example, the alternation between *o* and *a* in imperfective verbal derivation in Russian (e.g. *sprosít'* ~ *sprášivat'*) shows no phonological conditioning at all. Similarly, the alternation /f/ ~ /v/ in English 'wife' ~ 'wives', etc. is purely morphological. In both of these examples the conditioning, while morphological, is syntagmatic.

Having presented this brief classification, we should now take note of alternations which seem not to belong to either of the two major categories entirely, but rather straddle the two. Vowel reduction in Russian is one such alternation that deserves attention at this point. In Russian, unstressed non-diffuse vowels normally become diffuse and of high tonality (acute) when preceded by high tonality (palatalized or palatal) consonants; in other environments these same vowels tend to become neutral (i.e., [ʌ] or [ə]). There is no doubt that this is an automatic, purely phonological alternation in Russian, though there are complications. The alternation as described does not occur uniformly throughout inflectional endings: in certain desinential morphemes grammatical analogy will sometimes preserve a neutral /a/ in unstressed position where fronting and raising would be expected from an underlying stressed /á/ or /ó/. The analogy here is with /a/ and /o/ in the same inflectional suffixes when stressed. Interestingly enough, even though the analogical leveling has taken place, the regular sound change is also still a living process in the standard language, so that we have to do here with a genuine synchronically hybrid alternation. That such a thing should occur is not surprising, however, nor does it in any way invalidate the basic distinction we have been drawing between purely phonological and morphophonemic processes. Once again we can only reiterate that, especially in the mechanics of speech production, the division between functionally distinct levels is not always clear-cut. The lack of a clean break between the two levels in question here is simply a fact of language. As Jakobson has noted, "any intended comprehensive study of a phonemic pattern inevitably runs into the problem of partial patterns mutually distinguishing and specifying the diverse grammatical categories of a given language. The limit between phonemics proper and the so-called morphophonemics is more than labile. We glide from one to the other imperceptibly."[11]

The perspective I am outlining here is, of course, not new, nor is it original with Jakobson. It has a long tradition in Russian phonological theory beginning with Baudouin de Courtenay, who initiated the distinction between two types of alternations, which he termed "divergents" and "correlations". The first type included those alternants which differ only according to their phonological environment, while the second involved those whose conditioning was also morphological. This dichotomy was reiterated by Trubetzkoy, who distinguished between "combinatory" (automatic) and "free" (non-automatic) alternations, although in Trubetzkoy's analysis (especially of Slavic material) many automatic alternations ended up being classified as free because of a failure to realize the extent of the phonological regularity involved. It wasn't until Jakobson's pioneering work on "Russian Conjugation" in 1948 that the actual status of many of the alternations Trubetzkoy was working with was correctly identified through the positing of base forms to account for the actual phonological regularities. The contributions of each of these masters to the study of morphophonemics has been carefully set forth in a number of places by E. Stankiewicz, whose own work in the Slavic field continues this tradition in America.[12] In Soviet linguistics we find the same orientation expounded by the members of the so-called Moscow School of Phonology. As A. Reformatskij notes in his book on the history of Russian phonology, for example, the members of the Moscow School carefully distinguished between alternations of the type /k/ ~ /č/ in Russian in such verbal pairs is *peku ~ pečeš'* (1st sg. present ~ 2nd sg. present) — a true morphophonemic alternation that distinguishes, among other categories, the first person from other persons in the present tense of certain verbs — and purely phonological alternations such as that between /b/ and /p/ in /duba/ /dup/, which represents a straightforward neutralization of voicing in word final position.[13] Reformatskij's description of the differences between these two types of alternation is worth looking at for a moment in order to clarify the issues involved. He calls the first type a "traditional alternation of positionally independent separate phonemes," while the second he describes as a "positionally conditioned variation of one and the same phoneme." There is obviously in Reformatskij's formulation of the second type a vestige of the concept of archiphoneme: he sees in this type only one phoneme with positional variants, while the first type consists, in his formulation, of two separate phonemes. Such a description, however, does not adequately capture the essence of the difference, for the reasons already stated in Chapter 1. First, it poses the question of distinguishing between the two types at the phoneme level and not in terms of distinctive features. This gives the false impression that there is more of a difference between the /k/ and the /č/ of the first type than between the /b/ and the /p/ of the second, when in fact there is not. In **both** types there is a restriction on the occurrence of certain feature oppostions, and also in both types there **is** syntagmatic, contextual conditioning. In fact, it is precisely in the nature of the conditioning factors involved that the essence of the difference lies: the former contains morphological information which is absent in the latter. So while subscribing to the basic conclusion that we have to do with two different types of alternation, we can explain the distinction more accurately in other terms, explicitly invoking the qualitative difference in conditioning factors. This way the argument is not made on the basis of whether we have to do with one or two phonemes, which is very misleading because — as work in generative phonology has shown — one could just as well claim that there is only one phoneme in both cases.

Thus we may establish that the truly distinctive characteristic of the synchronic functioning of alternations is not the presence or absence of phonological conditioning, but rather the presence or absence of morphological conditioning, for when morphological conditioning is present, it indeed defines the essence of the alternation, and any other phonological conditioning that may also be present is secondary, and in fact is frequently of diachronic rather than synchronic import. We may view the process by which morphophonemic alternations develop historically in the following way. Most alternations originate as strictly phonological processes, as sound laws which at a certain moment no longer function as such synchronically in a particular language. Sound laws operate on purely phonological material and display more or less global patterning, but once they cease to function as such in a given language, the universality of their patterning begins to disintegrate, and what were once sound laws become alternations associated with specific classes of morphemes. It is at this point that we must reconsider their synchronic function and realize that the reason these sound patterns do not break up in a totally haphazard fashion, but instead continue to correspond fairly systematically with certain morphological categories, is that they have now assumed a morphological function. This is a perfectly logical development if we agree that, in principle, languages consistently strive to endow their formal elements with semantic values. The task of the linguist, then, is to capture the form-meaning relationships that such historical developments have generated in a given language.

The key to this approach is to be found once again in the sign function of language. Here meaning is not just one of several levels of analysis to be considered only at a certain point in the hierarchy of linguistic strata (as for example in such schemas as: phonology, morphology, syntax, **semantics**); rather, meaning is a function of all linguistic units at every level of analysis. Meaning in this sense is to be understood as the informational value of a form, and it is this semantic content that defines the functional essence of a form at whatever level it occurs. Applying this conception changes our perspective on the nature of formal units considerably: at every level in language we must ask ourselves what is the informational value of the form in question. At the strictly phonological level forms primarily give information only about themselves, i.e., a phoneme by itself tells us no more than that it is a sound distinct from other sounds in a specific language. A different type of information is provided when phonological oppositions are neutralized: the form in question provides information about neighboring sounds. Here the formal properties begin to assume some rudimentary grammatical functions, for already at this level we find sounds performing, for example, a demarcative function (e.g., neutralization of voicing in word-final position). In this case the informational content involves delimitation of word boundaries and the like: an intermediary stage in the linguistic hierarchy between the more general phonological and the more specific morphological functioning of speech sounds. In fact, at the boundary between these two levels we find a host of phonological elements which function in what we should call word phonology, delimiting the basic categories of roots and affixes. Here already phonemic patterning starts to become fragmented, and our description of the function of those phonological processes that operate within word phonology must reflect this partial patterning. From this point on in the linguistic hierarchy the function of speech sounds becomes increasingly selective and the writing of truly general rules less applicable. The only legimate role that general, purely phonological statements can play in word phonology and morphophonemics is a diachronic one, reflecting the historical source of alternations as previously functioning sound laws. The very fact that a sound law has ceased to operate is evidence that its synchronic function as a general phonological process no longer exists. To reconstruct such processes and claim synchronic relevance for them merely distorts our description of the actual synchronic structure of a language.

Once the study of morphophonemic relations has been established as a separate, relatively autonomous discipline, a whole series of observations about the nature of grammatical categories presents itself, observations about sound-meaning correspondences that would otherwise be completely ignored if the relations involved were treated as purely formal, phonological devices. We can illustrate how important it is not to obscure the relative autonomy of morphophonemic devices by returning for a moment to the Russian verbal system and in particular to the set of consonant mutations that accompanies vowel truncation. In Russian verbal paradigms consonants soften in one of two ways: either a hard consonant alternates with its palatalized counterpart (so-called 'bare' softening, e.g. /t/ ~ /t'/, /p/ ~ /p'/, etc.) or a more substantial shift takes place in which a velar or dental alternates with a palatal (termed 'subsitutive' or 'transitive' softening, e.g. /k/ ~ /č/, /d/ ~ /ž/, etc.). The alternations that occur may be stated as follows:

1. Suffixed –*i* and –*e* verbs have BARE softening throughout the verbal paradigm, except in the 1st sg. pres. where the softening is SUBSTITUTIVE.
2. Polysyllabic –*o* and –*a* verbs have SUBSTITUTIVE softening before all vocalic desinences.
3. Otherwise, BARE softening occurs before any vocalic desinence that does not begin with *u*.[14]

I have purposefully formulated these statements in such a way that, where relevant, they are made in phonological terms, but there is no attempt to increase the degree of formal generalization at the expense of morphological statements where the latter are themselves meaningful. From a purely phonological point of view, this may have the effect of making the rules seem at times ad hoc, but this impression ceases once one considers the broader spectrum of Russian verbal morphology and starts taking into account semantic as well as formal relationships. The phenomena described by this set of rules are true morphophonemic alternations. They occur systematically in the morphology of the verb – not only in the positions noted here, but also in imperfective derivation and participle formation – , but elsewhere their occurence is highly restricted, being limited to only a relatively few instances of nominal derivation and the comparative forms of certain adjectives. Their primary function is therefore clearly morphological rather than phonological, since elsewhere the presence of identical phonological conditions does not produce the alternations. Having observed that these particular processes participate in a distinctly partial patterning, we should therefore seek to determine their informational content, that is, with what grammatical concepts they are correlated. Some of the correlations will not be perfectly isomorphic, but this by itself in no way lessens the relevance of the correspondences observed between formal and meaningful constituents. On this point we can agree with Stankiewicz that because alternations frequently intersect with each other and with other grammatical devices (especially suffixes and desinences), such an ideal pattern is obviously precluded. And we may conclude, as Stankiewicz does, that "alternations do not so much carry distinctions between individual forms as sharpen the opposition between broader categories of forms (e.g. the singular vs. the plural, the direct cases vs. oblique cases, the past vs. the present, the pronoun vs. the noun)," and so forth.[15]

One of the morphological oppositions that is particularly highlighted by the consonantal alternations I have just described is that of the first person singular versus the other persons and numbers in the Russian verbal system. The presence of bare softening versus either substitutive softening or no softening at all corresponds fairly systematically with the morphological opposition between the other persons and numbers on the one hand and the first person singular on the other. In the suffixed *-i* and *-e* verbs (that is, all second conjugation verbs whose stems could undergo softening), the first person singular displays substitutive softening in contrast to the other personal desinences before which bare softening occurs. In all other verbs except the suffixed *-o* and *-a* stems (neither of which is productive, and which, taken together, comprise a total of only sixty verbs), bare softening occurs everywhere except before the first person singular and the third person plural, the two desinences that begin with *-u*. There are, furthermore, several other formal characteristics that are associated with the opposition of the first person singular to the rest of the verbal paradigm. First, the first singular is the only desinence that is composed of a single vowel phoneme; all the other personal desinences consist of at least a vowel plus a consonant. Second, the first singular is the only desinence that maintains the same phonological shape in both conjugations. And finally, if there is a stress alternation in the paradigm of the non-past tense, it will always oppose the first singular to the other persons and numbers. These observations take on additional significance when we realize that, of the three persons, the first person is the most semantically marked.[16] Since it is inconceivable that all of these correlations could be accidental, or merely historical remnants, we must conclude that they have an on-going functional significance in the language, and our linguistic description ought to reflect this fact.

3. OTHER FORMAL DEVICES IN MORPHOLOGY

As we noted at the outset of this chapter, the study of morphophonemics involves not only the analysis of alternations that serve a grammatical function, but is concerned with the totality of the formal devices that function in morphology. One of the most thorough illustrations of the scope of morphophonemics as defined herein was given by Jakobson in his treatment of Russian nominal inflection in "Morfologičeskie nabljudenija nad slavjanskim skloneniem."[17] This article presents an entire program of research into the morphophonemic structure of the Russian declensional system, and demonstrates in particular that the formal devices of language must always be investigated in the light of the semantic essence of the categories they delineate. Since this study has not yet appeared in any language but Russian, and since it contains a number of particularly programmatic statements, I will quote extensive portions of it here.

When investigating the phonological side of a language, we must inevitably take into consideration the grammatical entities within the confines of which specific sound laws operate. [. . .] The question then arises concerning the difference in sound structure of the various classes of grammatical entities — between root morphemes and different types of affixes, between stems and inflectional endings. Both the stems and desinences of each part of speech display characteristic differences in their sound structure which should be consistently delimited. For example, the specific inventory of phonemes and phoneme combinations must be established for the Russian inflectional endings in general, as well as for the conjugational and declensional desinences taken separately. Declensional inflection may be subdivided on the basis of dissimilarities in sound characteristics into substantival and adjectival patterns, while such grammatical categories as gender and number also specifically provide phonological features for the classification of the entire system (gender itself being in definite relation to declensional type). A structural analysis of the sound composition of the various endings of a given case of the same paradigm frequently provides the basis for determining the common phonological characteristics of that case. . . or of a class of cases.

Of special significance here is the question of case syncretism, i.e., the problem of loss of contrast between case endings and the order of such losses. No less important than complete syncretism in this respect and requiring as thorough an investigation is the question of partial syncretism. Here identity of desinences may be limited to only the existence of the same number of phonemes. . .or it may be limited to the common occurrence of only one of ɩ ιe phonemes in a set of desinences. [. . .]

The problem of how phonemes function within the confines of one or another morphological category, for example, within case inflection in general or just the singular or the plural, within the paradigms of a given grammatical gender, in a given class or merely in a given case, each involves the joint consideration of phonology and morphology. In singling out from the various polyphonemic endings of a given case or class of cases a common feature, specific to that one case or class of cases, we are converting the investigation of a grammatical form proper into an analysis of its phonological constitution. In this way the connection can be revealed between a case and its distinctive phoneme. . .and ultimately between the component elements of a case meaning and specific phonemes or component elements of phonemes. . . **Phonology and grammar prove to be indissolubly united by a whole series of transitional, interdisciplinary problems, the principle one of which is the indivisibility of linguistic sound and meaning.** (Bold type added.)

Thus we are confronted once again with the duality of the linguistic sign. The investigation of sound-meaning correspondences in morphology necessarily presupposes a semantic analysis of the morphological categories involved, which is to say that the study of the grammatical **processes** in a language has as its prerequisite the analysis of the set of grammatical **concepts** in that language. The study of grammatical processes matures only when the categories involved are not merely enumerated, but themselves are subjected to a thorough semantic analysis, which further study determines their linguistic essence. Only then can the true nature of the sound-meaning relationships in language be exposed. It is significant that the Nabljudenija begins with, and hence presupposes, a complete statement of the inherent semantic relationships by means of which the Russian case system is structured.[18] The formal analysis of grammatical processes, of which the bulk of the article is composed, is built upon this semantic material, as, for example, in the case of the observation that the bilabial nasal – in either of its two alternants, palatalized ~ unpalatized – is the mark of the 'marginal' cases (instrumental, dative, locative) and never occurs in any other case category.

Another study which complements the analysis presented in the Nabljudenija is "The Relationship between Genitive and Plural in the Declension of Russian Nouns."[19] Here we see that a number of formal peculiarities in the Russian declensional system, including the distribution of the zero desinences and certain analogical developments involving the prosodic pattern, can be explained and shown to be linguistically motivated if their occurrence is correlated with the semantic essence of the categories in which they appear. As a rule, the zero desinence in Russian nominal inflection is restricted to just two case forms, the nominative singular and genitive plural. In most declensional paradigms, the occurence of the zero desinence in one of these two forms alternates with a positive desinence in the other, so that, for example, if the nom. sg. ends in –*a* or –*o*, the gen. pl. will normally end in zero, and conversely, if the nom. sg. has a zero desinence, the desinence in the gen. pl. will be positive: –*ov* or –*ej*. This particular mode of expression, a quantitative opposition of a zero with a non-zero desinence, assumes special significance when it is realized that this formal opposition corresponds to a semantic opposition which itself has as its defining characteristic types of quantification: both the plural and the genitive case are quantifiers (See "Beitrag zur allgemeinen Kasuslehre"). Hence the contrast of gen. pl. and nom. sg. represents a confrontation of a twofold quantifier (genitive plus plural) with its doubly unmarked counterpart (nominative plus singular).

The intersection of grammatical categories that semantically involve quantifiers in the Russian nominal system presents yet another formal peculiarity, that of distinction by purely prosodic means, which most commonly occurs in the opposition of gen. sg. and nom. pl. Nouns with a non-zero desinence in the nom. sg. will have an identical desinence in both the gen. sg. and nom. pl. — nouns in *-a* have a gen. sg. and nom. pl. in *-i*; nouns in *-o* have a gen. sg. and nom. pl. in *-a* — and if these desinences are distinguished at all, it will be by placement of stress: specifically, an alternation of stress between stem and ending. Furthermore, nouns in *-a* show a gradual analogical extension of this stress alternation in the modern language, which demonstrates that this particular means of formal expression is quite alive. Likewise, masculine nouns with a nom. pl. in stressed *-a* oppose this desinence to unstressed *-a* in the gen. sg., and this alternation, too, is productive and rapidly expanding. As Jakobson notes, stress alternation is now used in the Russian declension only by quantifier cases.[20]

Clearly, if it were not for the semantic content invoked, the above observations would lose all of their force and become mere distributional catalogues of formal properties. The very life of language lies in the continual interplay of form and meaning, which two planes are not only intimately correlated, but frequently present us with striking similarities. The coincidence in the Russian declensional system between formal and semantic quantification should perhaps not be overemphasized, but this sort of correspondence is by no means an isolated phenomenon. Investigation into the degree to which sound and meaning units in languages reflect each other lie at the very frontier of linguistic research, and in this connection Jakobson has been one of the most persistent pioneers. His imaginative applications of the ideas of Charles Sanders Peirce on the nature of linguistic symbols, especially those concerning iconicity in language, must be counted among his most important recent studies.[21] These investigations are all the more meaningful in that they treat this potentially highly speculative subject matter as a thoroughly empirical problem, to be resolved with the utmost respect for the information contained in the primary data of individual languages. And in this same connection one cannot fail to mention the many studies of poetic language which, particularly in

Jakobson's post-Formalist maturity, consistently seek out the grammatical and other parallelisms that are associated with the more purely formal phenomena of sound repetition.[22]

But all this, as I have said, presupposes the semantic analysis of the morphologial categories involved, and it is to this study that we now turn.

CHAPTER THREE

Morphology

1. THE SIGN PRINCIPLE AS APPLIED TO THE STRUCTURE OF MEANING

In keeping with the principle of the linguistic sign, the structuration of abstract semantic elements mirrors quite closely that of the basic units of sound. In both instances we have to do with the conversion of foreign (extralinguistic) elements into linguistic values. Specifically, "language creates fixed phonemic units from the sound matter and fixed semantic units from the conceptual matter."[1] The parallel between these two processes is quite rigorous. According to Jakobson,

phonemes draw on sound matter but readjust this extrinsic matter, selecting, classifying, dissecting it along their own lines. Thus items of sound matter are transformed into semiotic elements. Likewise, languages draw meanings and semantic values from the intelligible world, from experience, but they readjust this extrinsic matter, selecting, dissecting, and classifying it along their own lines. Thus items of experience are transformed into semiotic entities.[2]

The essential linguistic process is one of conversion of extrinsic matter into a finite number of structured, intrinsically defined, linguistic abstractions. And it is through the sign function that this process of conversion is realized; for the abstraction of any invariant semantic quality from conceptual matter is always made strictly with regard to the existence of a specific formal category (or set of categories) in a given language, just as the abstraction of phonological invariance is always made with strict regard for the semantic function (meaning-distinguishing capacity) of the units in question: phonemes and ultimately distinctive features. In other words, the procedure for extracting invariance at each of the levels of sound and meaning is two-pronged: in phonology reference is made to both the physical properties of the signal and the semantic function of the qualities abstracted from the signal. Similarly, in semantic analysis invariant properties of meaning are defined in terms of both a certain range of contextual usage and a specific formal category with which the given range of usage is associated. This parallel application of the sign principle has been explicitly set forth by Jakobson, who insists that "the **semantic minimums** of a given language can be stated only with reference to their formal counterparts, and vice versa, the **minimal formal units** cannot be determined without reference to their semantic counterparts."[3] And again, "meaning can and must be stated in terms of linguistic discriminations and identifications, just as, on the other hand, linguistic discriminations are always made with regard to their semantic value."[4]

In semantics, therefore, the primary vehicle through which the extrinsic matter of experience is organized into an intrinsic linguistic structure is the set of sound forms (morphemes or larger formal constituents) extant in a particular language. Since it is the sound form which carries the meaning directly, it follows that there is no other means for distinguishing meanings than through the formal properties of sound. This principle, which I shall call the PRINCIPLE OF FORMAL DETERMINISM, can be stated succinctly in the following phrase: there is no *signatum* without *signum*. It is through the principle of formal determinism that we can establish the study of meaning as an intrinsically linguistic investigation, even though the material content of utterances has its ultimate source in external reality, just as we were able to establish an intrinsically linguistic science of phonology based upon a rigorous investigation of the physical properties of sounds made with systematic consideration of their semantic function. In each case the parallelism is complete: as the identification of linguistically relevant invariants of sound is semantically determined, so in like fashion the investigation of intrinsic linguistic invariance in semantic structure must be formally determined.

To appreciate more fully the rationale for an intrinsic science of meaning, we need to consider the relationship between meaning and reference.[5] If reference is the term used to designate the set of objects, or extra-linguistic phenomena, denoted by linguistic forms, then semantic analysis can be said to consist in some general sense of establishing the network of relationships between a given set of extra-linguistic objects (referents) and a set of forms in a given language. Furthermore, because this network of relationships is never in perfect equilibrium in any language — i.e., there is no isomorphic relationship between linguistic and extra-linguistic objects —, linguists and philosophers alike have found it exceedingly difficult to capture the essence of semantic structures. Jakobson has been able to establish the science of linguistic semantics on a substantially new footing in part by realizing that all along we have been looking at the referents of linguistic forms in the wrong light. The assumption has almost universally been made that, although the nature of **linguistic** objects may be relative rather than absolute, the referents of linguistic objects are themselves absolute. Consider for example, the problematics involved in the oft-cited distinction between "morning star" and "evening star," which is commonly evoked as an instance of two different linguistic objects referring to one and the same extra-linguistic object. Under such an interpretation, the existence of the planet Venus is taken to be the single, absolute referent of both linguistic expressions. It is in just this interpretation, however, that Jakobson does not concur, for in his view, it is not the existence of the planet that is being referred to, but rather "two different phases of the appearance of the planet."[6] We know this because we cannot substitute the one expression for the other in every situation.

It is central to Jakobson's insight into the nature of reference that "every object always appears in a situation, in a network of relations that is defined temporally, spatially, or by its content and that must be taken into account in determination of the referent. We cannot designate an object without, at the same time, introducing it into a situation or a context."[7] Thus the strictly relational nature of the objects referred to by language is set forth as a principle, and as a result, the study of linguistic form and meaning assumes a significantly different character. If we agree that reference is a relational or contextual (situational) phenomenon, then the traditional distinction between meaning and reference can be transposed into one considerably easier to deal with, namely the distinction between general and contextual meaning. This transposition has the advantage of putting both aspects – the invariant and its variations – in the same sphere instead of operating between two different spheres: linguistic and extra-linguistic reality.[8] Jakobson explicitly makes this trans-position; in fact, he insists that the meaning of any word is necessarily a **semiotic** fact which cannot possibly be inferred from a non-linguistic acquaintance with objects.

No one can understand the word 'cheese' unless he has an acquaintance with the meaning assigned to this word in the lexical code of English. [. . .] The meaning of the word 'cheese' cannot be inferred from a non-linguistic acquaintance with cheddar or with camembert without the assistance of the verbal code. [. . .] Mere pointing will not teach us whether **cheese** is the name of the given specimen, or of any box of camembert, or of cam-embert, in general, or of any cheese, any milk product, any food, any re-freshment, or perhaps any box irrespective of contents.[9]

This is because there is no such thing as an "absolute 'thing in itself,' no x which can be completely detached from its modes of givenness."[10] And because of this fact, meaning cannot be de-fined on objects in external reality, but must be defined rather on the set of signs in a given language, and therefore ultimately on linguistic form.

At the same time, however, it should be made clear that this perspective on the nature of linguistic meaning does not divorce meaning from reference. As always, the autonomy being pro-posed is relative. What we have to understand is that languages draw meanings from external reality, but they reorganize this extrinsic matter, each language somewhat differently, into an essentially subjective system of symbols. Semantic analysis is therefore not the study of the properties of referents – this is the province of the physical scientist – , but rather the study of the subjective reordering of external reality by a given language. In other words, the set of objects that the linguist is investigating is one step removed from that of the physicist. Here lies the essential difference between linguistics and the physical sciences: "The stimuli received from Nature. . .are not pictures of reality but are the evidence from which we build our personal models. While the physicist creates his historical construct, imposing his own hypothetical system of new symbols upon the extracted **indices**, the linguist only recodes, translates into symbols of a metalanguage those extant **symbols** which are used in the language of the given speech community."[11]

If there is any doubt about this essential difference in ontological status of linguistic meaning as opposed to reference, it is sufficient to remember that one can create by means of language imaginary situations and even objects that do not exist in the real world at all; and one can also lie with language. This aspect of linguistic creativity is an essential property of language. The non-existence or fictitiousness of such things as ambrosia or green ideas has no bearing on the question of their semantic significance. As long as the grammatical relations of a sentence remain intact, the meaning of any utterance will be interpretable within the semantic system of the language in which it is uttered. Both ambrosia and green ideas can be submitted to a truth test because the problem of truth in language "is not the correspondence between a meaning and a reference, but rather the compatibility between two meanings, two modes of givenness, or two contextual determinations."[12]

The question of truth or existence, as Jakobson sees it, can only be raised in relation to a context. Every indefinite existential utterance – 'Ambrosia exists.' 'Quarks exist' – is an elliptical utterance requiring completion by an indication of which system of meanings it is operative in. Ambrosia exists in the framework of Greek mythology. And within this framework, not only meaningful but also true and untrue statements can be made about ambrosia. The gods eat ambrosia, they don't drink it.[13]

Likewise, with respect to Chomsky's famous sentence, "Color-less green ideas sleep furiously," we may ask:

Do things like colorless green, green ideas, sleepy ideas, or a furious sleep exist or not? 'Colorless green' is a synonymous expression for 'pallid green' with a slight epigrammatic effect of an apparent oxymoron. The metaphoric epithet in 'green ideas' is reminiscent of Andrew Marvell's famous 'green thought in a green shade' and of the Russian idiom 'green boredom' (*zelenaja skuka*) or of Tolstoj's 'horror red, white and square' (*vse tot že užas krasnyj, belyj, kvadratnyj*). In its figurative sense, the verb 'sleep' means to 'be in a state like sleep, as that of inertness, torpidity, numbness,' e.g. 'his hatred never slept;' why, then, cannot someone's ideas fall into sleep? And finally, why cannot the attribute 'furious' emphatically render a frenzy of sleep?[14]

Instead, therefore, of operating with the concepts of meaning and reference, the sign theory of language approaches semantic analysis rather from the point of view of general vs. contextual meaning. In analyzing the meaning of a given form, the linguist studies the full range of contextual usage associated with the form in question in order to abstract from this range of contextual material an invariant, common denominator of meaning. The semantic common denominator is the general meaning of the form, which is both implied by and itself implies the existence of specific contextual variants. The parallel with phonemic analysis is clear: "Linguistic meanings are differential in the same sense that phonemes are differential sound units. A linguist knows that speech sounds present, besides phonemes, contextual and optional situational variants (or under other labels, 'allophones' and 'metaphones'). Correspondingly, on the semantic level we observe contextual meanings and situational meanings. But variations cannot be acknowledged without the existence of invariants."[15]

The reciprocal implication of general and contextual mean-ing – i.e., of the generic and the specific – lies at the very core of semantic analysis. The relationship between general and contextual meaning displays the same essentially RELATIONAL and TOPOLOGICAL nature that characterizes phonological invariance.[16] The invariant semantic common denominator of a form is that property or set of properties which remains constant throughout all the specific contextual applications of the form. The general meaning of a form is truly generic in character: it is a Gesamtbedeutung as opposed to a Grundbedeutung, a property or set of properties present in all the usages of the form and not just in its most common or frequently occurring applications. As Jakobson put it, "any symbol is endowed with general meaning, and the general meaning of any symbol, and of any verbal symbol in particular, has a generic character. Any further segmentation and individuation of the symbol is determined by its context. Thus **tree** means any species and any individual instance of a kind of plant, and only a context can adapt this word to one single species or to one single specimen."[17]

For a formulation of the essentially generic character of meaning we may turn, as Jakobson does, to the reasoning of the American philosopher Charles Sanders Peirce.[18] For Peirce, a genuine symbol is a symbol which has a general meaning, In fact, a symbol is incapable of indicating a particular thing, but necessarily denotes a kind of thing. A symbol, for instance a word, is a general rule which signifies only through the different instances of its application. However varied these applications of the word, it remains in all its occurrences one and the same word. Furthermore, it is upon the symbol as a general rule that the creative use of language is predicated, for the mode of being of a symbol consists in the real fact that something surely will be experienced if certain conditions are satisfied, namely that the symbol be placed in a specific contextual situation. The primary value of a symbol for Peirce is its potential: a truly general law cannot be fully realized; it is a potentiality, and its mode of being is *esse in futuro*. It is precisely the potentiality of the linguistic sign, that is, the general meaning which constitutes its essence, that guarantees we will be able to understand someone else's use of, or use ourselves, a familiar word in an entirely novel situation. That we are able to create and understand new contexts when we hear them "is proof that the constituents of such a context are known to us and possess an invariant semantic value."[19]

Let us now proceed to illustrate the application of these

concepts to one area of semantic investigation, namely to the analysis of grammatical meaning. We will have occasion later to distinguish between grammatical and lexical meaning as separate types of categories based upon their unique semantic properties. It is appropriate to concentrate first on the analysis of grammatical meaning if only because the range of semantic variability is here considerably more circumscribed than in lexical meaning. The following section will be devoted primarily to the analysis of meaning in the Russian case system as presented by Jakobson in two studies, the "Beitrag zur allgemeinen Kasuslehre" of 1936, and the "Morfologičeskie nabljudenija nad slavjanskim skloneniem" of 1958. This analysis is especially noteworthy because it is the first to have actually succeeded in isolating and defining a set of invariant recurring semantic features, consideration of which will allow us to establish some further principles of semantic analysis as corollaries to the ones discussed in this section.

2. INTRODUCTION TO GRAMMATICAL MEANING: THE RUSSIAN CASE SYSTEM

The problem of the general meaning of case forms is the central issue posed by Jakobson in his analysis of grammatical meaning in the Russian case system. Specifically he is concerned with establishing the inseparability of a grammatical form and its function, i.e., of "the unity of a grammatical category [and] the unity of its meaning."[20] In the study of grammatical meaning the critical problem is to avoid separating the concept of grammatical category either from its "phonetically realized grammatical form" or from its "meaning in the language, which makes it distinct from every other category."[21] The establishment of invariance at the level of grammatical meaning is a topological question of determining "those properties of each given morphological category which remain unchanged throughout all the contextual variations of that category," or, put more precisely, it is the study of "the invariant relationship between two opposing morphological categories, which relationship remains independent of the occurrence of these categories in one or another lexical or syntactic environment."[22]

Though other linguists have perceived the importance of this issue, few have posed the problem of invariance in grammatical meaning with the clarity or consistency of Jakobson, and none before him has seen its solution so explicitly. Consider, for example, the early twentieth-century Russian linguist Peškovskij, who specifically voiced concern over the fragmentation of meanings that results when the unity of a given case category is not preserved.

Since the meanings of cases are closely related to the referential meanings of the governors and the subordinate words, the investigator is tempted to set up as many parameters as can be found for the referential meanings of each of the concatenated elements and to add more parameters for their various combinations. Thus once an investigator establishes, let us say, the meaning of INSTRUMENTALITY [*orudnost'*] for the instrumental case [in Russian] in phrases such as *rubit' toporom* ['to chop with an axe'] and *pilit' piloj* ['to saw with a saw'], he may discern a new meaning in the phrases *sxvatyvat' mysl'ju* ['to grasp mentally'], *čujat' serdcem* ['to feel with one's heart'], or *ponimat' umom* ['to understand in one's mind'], for in these cases the 'instrument' as well as what it does are entirely different. And then the analyst may discern still another meaning in the phrases *dejstvovat' podkupom* ['to act by bribery'], *dobivat' sja čego siloj, terpeniem* ['to try to achieve something by force, by patience'] or *očarovyvat' kogo ostroumiem* ['to charm someone by one's wit']. In the first case one could refer to a case of 'mental instrument', in the second to a case of 'means',. . . When one adopts this course, there is no limit to the fragmentation of meanings (for example, one could distinguish between 'mental' and 'emotional' instruments, between 'physical, economic, and social' means, and so on).[23]

Peškovskij's concern again points up the strictly relational character of referential meanings and demonstrates the need for defining semantic invariance on something other than the properties of referents. Yet Peškovskij's own solution itself falls short of the goal of establishing a truly general meaning for a grammatical category. He posits instead a "composite of meanings"

[*ob'edinennyj komplex*] for a single grammatical case whenever
the unity of the case meaning is not to him intuitively clear.
The resulting semantic composite consists of different meanings
which themselves have nothing in common.[24] Thus, for example,
the Russian instrumental case in his system is defined by no less
than eleven separate meanings, the 'instrumentality' discussed in
the quote above being but one of the eleven. Furthermore, the
only methodological principle Peškovskij offers for determining
what is the correct set of such meanings for a given case is the
following: "One does not establish more meanings than are absolutely necessary for the explanation of one or another fact."[25]
The resulting subjectivity of the list of meanings arrived at by
this method for a given case is a fact that cannot be overlooked.
The problem here, of course, is the classic one of determining
upon what ultimately to base judgments of sameness and difference in meaning. Peškovskij and others have realized that the
question cannot be resolved by investigating referential meanings
because here we find only differences, and this inevitably leads
us into a vicious relativity. At the same time, however, Peškovskij
is unwilling to go so far as to systematically posit truly general
meanings, meanings as unified as the formal categories they correspond with, since in many instances the contextual applications
of a given form appear to be too disparate, too heterogeneous
to justify subsuming them under a single invariant of meaning.

Jakobson, on the other hand, **is** willing to take this critical
step, not only because such a concept of invariance is thoroughly
consistent with linguistic sign theory, but also because it is
strongly supported by concepts outside of linguistics, independently arrived at by theoreticians in a variety of disciplines,
including philosophy, mathematics, and psychology.[26] We have
already considered the connection with mathematics, in the discussion of the sense in which invariants at both the levels of
sound and meaning are topological invariants.[27] The notion of
topological invariant is also consistent with the concept of
Gestalt quality in psychology. Both are intimately concerned
with considerations of parts and wholes, which in one sense can
be applied to the relationship between an invariant semantic

quality and its diverse contextual variants. The notion that the whole – the Gestalt or invariant – is more than the sum of its parts rests on the observation, common to many disciplines, that "a whole has properties that its parts, taken individually, do not have. Harmony and rhythm are properties of a sequence of notes but never of an isolated note. . . The transummative qualities of a Gestalt (Übersummativität) can be transferred to **entirely different multiplicities of elements without affecting the Gestalt quality**. It remains invariant as opposed to its variable parts."[28]

In this sense the parallel with phonology can be most instructive. As we noted above (p. 18), compactness in the French system of consonants displays three contextual variants, each determined by a concurrent feature: compact consonants are realized as velar when plosive, as palatal when nasal, and as postalveolar when continuant. Despite the considerable diversity of contextual realizations, the relative compactness remains invariant. In other words, the purely abstract relations remain unchanged, unaffected by even the most disparate concrete (in this case articulatory) applications.[29] Exactly the same type of relation holds in semantics, as for example in the analysis of case meanings, where "each case displays in its various applications a set of more or less heterogeneous meanings. The differences between each of these specific, contextual meanings are definable either by the grammatical or the lexical composition of the environment in which the case occurs. . . Whatever the diversity of semantic variants, dependent upon purely syntactic or lexical conditions, the unity of the case itself remains real and inviolable."[30] Thus, "all the specific contextual meanings of any case can be reduced to a common denominator. In relation to the other cases of the same declensional system, every case is characterized by its own invariant general meaning."[31] Consider the following example:

The morphological invariant in the semantics of the Russian genitive [G] is readily extractable from the wealth of contextual variants associated with it. The G retains its general meaning in whatever variation it is found, which general meaning distinguishes this case from both the nominative [N] and the accusative [A] cases. There is always present in the G a tendency towards limitation of participation by the object in the contents of the utterance. The G always signalizes the degree of objectivity of the object in the given context, and only the context determines, specifies what in fact these limits are. The presence of the object may be measured (*skol'ko, stol'ko-to novostej* 'how much, so much news'), heightened (*novostej!* 'What news!' or *naslušalis' novostej* 'got an earful of news'), limited (*poslušali, kosnulis' novostej* 'listened to, concerned some news'), reduced to potential state (*ždali, xoteli, iskali novostej* 'waited for, hoped for, looked for news'), or reduced to null (*ne slyxali novostej* 'didn't hear any news' or *ne bylo novostej* 'there was no news'). Finally, the presence of the object can be averted or rejected (*izbegali, pugalis' novostej* 'avoided, were frightened by the news'). The substantival G denotes that what is involved in the utterance is not the whole object, nor the object per se, but only a part or property of it, its action, its state, or objects related to it (*obryvki, zanimatel'nost', vlijanie, vozniknovenie, peredača, istočnik, slušatel' novostej* 'excerpts, fascination, effect, origin, transmission, source, hearer of (the) news')[32]

This is one sense, then, in which the concept of general meaning corresponds to notions of relational invariance independently motivated and developed in other disciplines.

There is yet another aspect of this conceptualization of semantic invariance which is supported by parallel concepts in adjacent disciplines as well as in phonology. That is the sense in which invariants of meaning are defined not in isolation from each other, but are themselves terms of relation, such that each invariant exists only by virtue of its opposition to the other invariants within the same system. Up to this point, in talking about the relational nature of semantic invariance, we have been primarily concerned with the relationship between specific and general meanings, but semantic invariance is also relational in the sense that the general meanings themselves can only be defined in terms of the total set of general meanings that constitutes the semantic structure of a given language. Here the same problem of parts and wholes is simply being posed at another level: an element with a holistic character at one level itself becomes part of a larger whole at the next highest level. Like distinctive features of sound, the ultimate semantic minimums of language are thus partial wholes whose constitution depends upon the other elements of the same system for their definition. Thus the relational structure of semantic invariants within a given linguistic system specifically displays a network of OPPOSITIONS, much the same as in phonology, where we find we must operate ultimately with pairs of oppositive terms. The linguistic structure of both sound and meaning exhibits, in fact, a special type of opposition, that of binary relations where one element necessarily evokes the other. Furthermore, the binary relations observed are not just constructs of the linguist, but are actual artifacts of language. As the Dutch phenomenologist H.J. Pos insists:

Opposition. . .is a principle of structure. It always unites two things which are distinct, but at the same time connected in such a way that thought cannot posit the one without the other. The unity of opposites is always formed by a concept which implicitly contains them in itself and becomes divided into an explicit opposition when it is applied to concrete reality. . . Opposition in linguistic facts is not a scheme which science has introduced to master the facts and which remains external to them. Its import surpasses the epistemological sphere: when linguistic thought orders facts according to the principles of opposition and system, it encounters a thinking which itself creates these facts.[33]

In phonology, the existence of oppositive relations provides the basis for analysis in terms of distinctive features. One cannot define a phoneme without reference to the other phonemes of the same linguistic system. In order to accomplish this task, one must break down phonemes into their ultimate component parts, which parts — or features — are the discrete, differential properties that constitute the essence of the given sound system. A phoneme by itself does not imply or predict any other particular phoneme in a given language; it is only the differential properties of distinctive features that oppose one phoneme to another. A /t/ in Russian does not by itself imply any other phoneme in the language, but the presence of the feature voicing, for example, does imply that there are pairs of phonemes in the language in which the presence versus absence of voicing can serve to distinguish meaning.

Likewise, in semantics, we analyze a given morpheme into a bundle of features representative of the several components that make up its general meaning and that relate that meaning to the meanings of the other morphemes within the same grammatical or lexical category. Within the case system of Russian, for example, the accusative [A] and dative [D] are opposed to the nominative [N] and instrumental [I] respectively by the presence of the marking 'directionality' in the former vs. its absence in the latter.[34] Similarly, the I and D are opposed to the N and A by the presence of the feature 'marginality'. The resulting relationship among these four cases can be diagrammed as follows, where the points on the top side of the square are marked for 'directionality' (vs. those on the bottom), and the points on the right side are marked for 'marginality' (vs. those on the left).

Thus the N is the doubly unmarked case, the A being opposed to it by the marking of 'directionality' and the I by 'marginality'; the D is marked for both features. Continuing the analysis to include the remaining cases in the Russian declensional system requires the postulation of one additional feature, 'quantification'. By this marking the two genitives [GI] and [GII] and the two locatives [LI] and [LII] are opposed to the first four cases above; while the locatives are opposed to the genitives again by marking of 'marginality', and each of the locatives and each of the genitives themselves are distinguished by 'directionality'. Thus the full set of case relationships may be represented graphically in the form of a cube, simply be adding a second square to the rear of the original one.

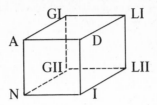

Points on the back side of the cube are marked for 'quantification' (vs. those on the front), and the rest of the relations remain the same.

The schematic representation that I have adopted here from the Nabljudenija displays the set of case relationships in their most graphic form. The use of such a graph provides an explicit visual representation of the semantic correlations that the general meaning of a given case participates in, and an immediate recognition of the set of minimal oppositions that distinguish one case from others in the same system. It is readily apparent from the diagram above, for instance, that the I is most directly related to the N by the presence of the marking 'marginality', to the D as the unmarked member of a 'directionality' correlation, and to the LII as the unmarked member of the correlation of 'quantification'.

Though I have not been concerned in this study with the respect in which Jakobson's approach represents a phenomenology of language, a point ought to be made at this juncture of the extent to which his analysis of meaning in the Russian case system makes a substantial contribution to phenomenological theory. Similar to approaches in other disciplines which seek to determine the relational nature of abstract invariants, phenomenology, particularly in its Husserlian variety, is concerned with uncovering the immanent structural laws that constitute the essence of an object. Husserl's program contained a call for determining both the "invariant essential traits" of an object and the "network of relations" that bind that object to others in the same field of experience and beyond. But, as Holenstein notes, the latter part of this program, especially as it concerns meaning, remained unfulfilled in Husserl's life work. It is to Jakobson that we owe the

empirical solution to the problem of relational invariance in semantic structure.

Husserl was made famous by his theory of eidetic abstraction, aimed at
uncovering the invariant essential traits of an object or a meaning. In the
process he came to the conclusion that the extrication of the consistently
invariant features of a single object did not suffice to characterize it fully.
It must additionally be placed in relation first to the objects of the category
or region to which it belongs and then to the totality of categories, to
the world in its entirety. This insight largely remained only a postulate in
Husserl. His eidetic analyses are atomistically restricted to single objects.
The invariant network of relations, within which each object is constituted,
remained largely unstudied. Herein lies Jakobson's contribution to eidetic
phenomenology, as it is called, which seeks to uncover the eidetic univer-
salities of an object or a region of objects. Jakobson succeeded in demonstrating how a range of objects can be described by a harmonious system
of relational features. The cosmos of ideas is no hodgepodge of data that
can only be 'savoured' individually. It is a well-ordered system.[35]

If Jakobson is right, and such a grammatical category as case
does display the remarkable relational symmetry his analysis
suggests, then we should expect to find features similar to the
ones he has isolated recurring in other grammatical categories of
the Russian language, and in categories of lexical meaning and
word formation as well. In fact, this is just what van Schooneveld
has succeeded in demonstrating, and we shall consider his contribution shortly. For the moment, however, there remain several methodological considerations about the nature of semantic
oppositions that still require elaboration.

3. STRUCTURAL DIFFERENCES BETWEEN PHONOLOGICAL AND
   MORPHOLOGICAL OPPOSITIONS

There are certain respects in which semantic oppositions differ
from phonological oppositions and where simply borrowing
concepts from the one discipline to the other can lead to serious
misunderstanding of the nature of semantic invariance. One of
these concerns the fact that, whereas phonological oppositions

are purely distinctive in character, grammatical – and in general, semantic – oppositions do have a meaning of their own.[36] A phoneme by itself means nothing; it is, as Sausssure would say, a purely relative, oppositive, and negative entity. And, as the Prague theoreticians noted, the phoneme signifies "mere otherness". Morphemes, on the other hand, – and, by extension, morphological oppositions – are not merely distinctive, but are endowed with their own meaning. A morpheme always signifies something, even when it occurs in isolation or in a context where no opposition is possible. In other words, at the morphological (semantic) level of language, entities are not purely relative, oppositive, **and negative**, but always retain their constant general meaning, which is their positive and necessary attribute.

Phonemes by themselves have no meaning: the pair /t/ : /d/ is correlated with the other consonants of the same linguistic system by the opposition unvoiced : voiced. These two phonemes can serve as the distinguishing characteristic of two otherwise identical grammatical units. . . In application to the morphological plane the occasion can easily arise for misunderstanding Saussure's thesis that, 'pris isolément ni *Nacht* ni *Nächte* ne sont rien: donc tout est opposition.' Obviously, the relation *Nacht* : *Nächte* presupposes the presence of the opposition of the grammatical categories singular and the plural in the code of the German language. So long as such an opposition is given, the form *Nächte*, taken in isolation, itself implies 'more than one night', whereas both /t/ and /d/ by themselves, in fact, 'ne sont rien.'[37]

This observation assumes special significance when it comes to determining the semantic nature of a morpheme which occurs in a context where no opposttition is possible – as, for example, when only one case form can occur in a particular syntactic combination. Verbal government in Russian (and any number of other inflecting languages) provides innumerable instances of this type of limited syntactic distribution of cases. All too frequently it is claimed that such instances represent a purely syntactic – and therefore "semantically empty" – use of case forms. If, on the other hand, we do not a priori assume that in such combinations the one case that does occur has no meaning, but rather that the meaning of a form remains intact in all its contextual applications, then we find that the instances of syntactic restriction themselves can be explained as a factor of semantic compatibility between the grammatical meaning of the case form and the lexical meaning of the verb.

To illustrate the point, consider two of the verbs of 'using' in Russian: *upotrebljat'*, which takes only A objects, and *pol'zovat'sja*, which governs objects only in the I. The first of these two verbs typically occurs in the following types of situations; (1) to denote the use of a particular kind of verbal construction, e.g., *upotrebljat' vyraženie, oborot, čast' reči, aforizm, glagol* 'to use an expression, turn of phrase, part of speech, aphorism, verb'; (2) to denote types of ingredients used in cooking, e.g., *upotrebljat' sladkoe, mjasco, moločnye produkty* 'to use (cook with) sweets, meat, milk products'; and (3) in such instances as *upotrebljat' vlast', usilija, ènergiju* 'to use (one's) authority, effort, energy'. What each of these types has in common is a kind of usage which completely involves the object, such that the object is either "used up", as in cooking or in using one's strength or energy, or it is otherwise directly manipulated by the process, as when one uses a word, part of speech, and the like. Significantly, the A case, which is the only case that occurs with this verb, is marked for one feature, directionality, which in Jakobson's definition implies the direct or total involvement of the object in the verbal process.

On the other hand, the verb *pol'zovat'sja* governs objects only in the I, the case marked for the feature of marginality. In contrast to the first verb, *pol'zovat'sja* invariably denotes situations where the object remains relatively unaffected by the action of the verb: objects of *pol'zovat'sja* are marginal to the process in the sense that they are mere instruments. Typical complements of this verb are, for example, means of transportation: *pol'zovat'sja avtobusom, tramvaem, liftom* 'to use a bus, trolley, elevator'. Objects that occur with *pol'zovat'sja* are not directly involved in the verbal process in the sense that objects of *upotrebljat'* are, for their status is not altered as a result of the process: e.g. *pol'zovat'sja pračečnoj, stolovoj, počtoj, xolodil'-nikom, britvoj, slovarem, melom* 'to use the laundry, dining hall, post office, refrigerator, razor, dictionary, piece of chalk.'[38] This verb can also be used in the specific contextual meaning of 'enjoy' in the sense of 'profit from': e.g. *pol'zovat'sja uspexom (u zritelej), ljubov'ju (u detej), podderžkoj, uvaženiem (u kogo–to)* 'to enjoy success (before an audience), the love (of one's children), the support, respect (of someone)'. Here it is more the subject that receives the effect of the process than the instrumental complement.

(It might be wise to digress here for a moment and note, in deference especially to the reader who knows Russian well, that the range of usage illustrated in this set of examples is, of course, somewhat limited, and that this limitation can give the impression that the examples chosen do not adequately represent the full extent of contextual variation associated with the categories in question. Moreover, in presenting an admittedly limited set of data such as this, the impression may be left that the analysis is not coming from the data so much as it is being imposed upon them. Unfortunately, I can see no way of avoiding these problems in a book such as this without doubling the size of the text and engaging in an extensive presentation of data that would be well beyond the scope of this study. In fact, a detailed exposition of contextual case usages was presented by Jakobson in his 1936 article, and I see no particular value in repeating this material here. Instead, I have made a point of citing examples that clarify the use of these features as consistently as possible throughout the remainder of this book, so that by the final chapter the reader should have a clear picture of the concepts involved.)

We should also take note at this point of the sort of evidence that is frequently adduced against the assertion that formal distinctions such as that between the accusative and instrumental cases can be correlated so systematically with conceptual invariants. The most frequently suggested evidence involves those instances where two formally distinct categories both participate in expressions which appear to have the same meaning. In Russian, for example, one can say either *pol'zovat'sja slovom* (I) or *upotrebljat' slovo* (A) with roughly the same meaning: 'use a word'. And if a native speaker of Russian is simply asked, without further specification of a context, if these two expressions differ in meaning, the answer will probably be no. One must, however, be careful how one utilizes native intuitions in cases like this which, of course, occur all the time. I would like to suggest that this sort of apparent semantic overlapping is very much the same phenomenon we saw with so-called phonemic overlapping. (For an important difference between phonological and conceptual features, however, see immediately below.) Both of these types of overlapping display a coalescence of the absolute physical properties outside of language, not of the strictly relative properties of language itself. As I noted above, the distinctive features represent oppositive values that situate themselves on a sliding scale, so to speak, of absolute phonetic facts. By the same token, the semantic distinctions that are codified in language are relative and oppositive entities which have as one of their most important characteristics the ability to refer to different aspects of one and the same external phenomenon. Thus any number of different linguistic constructions – such as the active and passive, for example – often appear to have the same referent, and they may indeed refer to the same absolute physical phenomenon, but the referential capability that is built in to our linguistic competence (see above, pages 49ff) is in no way restricted to the specification of existential, real-world properties. Hence whether an active and a corresponding passive construction will refer to the same concrete situation or not, is properly viewed as a matter of performance, for we find just as many specific situations where the two may not be used interchangeably as we do instances where they may. Likewise, when the meaning of utterances such as *pol'zovat'sja slovom* and *upotrebljat' slovo* is investigated to its fullest extent and the native informant is asked if he cannot conceive of contexts where one of the expressions would be permissable and the other not, one invariably begins to uncover a difference in meaning. In testing out the difference in the ranges of contextual application of these two utterances, I have been struck by the consistency with which native speakers conclude that the accusative occurs when the context is "rather formal or specific," whereas the instrumental usage is "more general," which is precisely what the difference between directionality and marginality would suggest: with the instrumental case the verbal complement assumes a more adverbial function, while the accusative stresses an action directed towards a specific goal. Ultimately, what one usually finds in such cases are preferences for one usage over another in particular contexts rather than absolute prohibitions of usage: one of the utterances will sound better in a certain context, though the context itself may not be sufficient to force the choice. One is much more likely to encounter the accusative usage *upotrebljat' slovo*, for example, in a situation where a student had had difficulty learning a word and finally began to use it properly, but the instrumental could also occur.

We cannot conclude, therefore, that the difference in meaning between two formally distinct grammatical categories is ever completely neutralized. Nor are we justified in assuming that the kind of verbal government illustrated here can be treated as a purely formal, syntactic phenomenon. To do so is to ignore the systematic signifying function of formal units. In fact, the observations made here point up the importance of looking to the inherent semantic content present in every form for the explanation of a wide range of syntactic phenomena which are frequently wrongly considered merely formal properties. Even such syntactic combinations as the use of a case with certain prepositions in no way deprives the case form of its constant meaning, even when, following a given preposition, there is no choice of case.

Though it happens that in certain contexts the use of a given case is compulsory and that in this instance its meaning turns out to be redundant, this circumstance does not allow us to equate even so predictable a meaning with meaninglessness. It would be a sheer misunderstanding to imagine that these occasional redundancies might invalidate to any extent the search for the general meanings of grammatical cases. It is true that the Russian preposition *k* 'to' implies the dative case, but the Russian dative does not imply an antecedent preposition *k* and thus preserves its own general meaning of 'direction toward' [= marked for directionality and marginality], just as the Russian noun *xleb* 'bread' does not lose its meaning when preceded by the adjective *peklevannyj* 'whole meal', though *xleb* is the only noun one can expect after this attribute.[39]

Grammatical and phonological oppositions differ significantly in this respect.

In a sequence of two English obstruents, if the first is voiceless, the second too must be voiceless: [kukt] 'cooked'. In this instance,...the apparent analogy between the grammatical and phonemic sequences is misleading. Redundancy does deprive the phonemic feature of its distinctiveness, but it cannot rob meaningful units of their proper sense.[40]

In other words, phonemic oppositions, because they are purely distinctive in character, may be contextually neutralized, whereas morphemic oppositions, which are endowed with their own meaning, are not neutralizable in this sense. When the distinctive function of a phonemic opposition is contextually removed, nothing else remains, and we are correct in saying that the opposition is neutralized. But removing the purely distinctive function of a morphemic opposition still leaves its inherent meaning intact, and we should not speak of neutralization in such a case.

Semantic oppositions differ from phonological oppositions in yet another respect, viz. in the very nature of the oppositions themselves — i.e., in the nature of the relationship between a marked and a corresponding unmarked category. In phonology we have to do with two entities which are correlated with each other by the presence vs. the absence of a particular distinguishing feature (e.g. voiced vs. unvoiced, nasal vs. non-nasal). Semantic correlations, on the other hand, display a different kind of relationship. In morphology, the general meaning of a marked form signals the presence of a particular semantic quality, but the general meaning of the corresponding unmarked form does not signal the absence of that quality, nor does it signal the presence of the opposite quality. Rather, the general meaning of an unmarked form simply provides no information about either the presence or absence of the marking in question, and only the context of the unmarked form determines whether the quality is present or not.

In studying two distinct morphological categories, one often proceeds on the assumption that the two categories have equal status, that each has its own positive meaning: Category I means *x*, Category II means *y*; or at least I means *x*, and II means the absence or negation of *x*. In reality the general meanings of correlative categories are distributed differently: if Category I denotes the presence of *x*, then Category II does **not** denote the presence of *x* — that is, Category II does not signify whether *x* is present or not. The general meaning of Category II with respect to Category I is limited to the lack of the '*x*-signal'.

When Category II in a given context announces the absence of *x*, this is merely a contextual application of the given category: here the meaning is conditioned by the situation, and even if it is the most common function of this category, linguists should not equate the statistically preponderant meaning of the category with its general meaning.[41]

As an example of a typical grammatical opposition, consider the relationship between singular and plural in a language like Russian. The plural in Russian is clearly marked vs. the singular: it always designates more than one of the phenomenon in question. The singular is unmarked with respect to the plural: the general meaning of the singular simply does not stipulate whether there is one or more of the object present. The Russian phrase *interes k dramam* (pl.) 'interest in (the) dramas' necessarily implies more than one drama; but *interes k drame* (sg.) may in different contexts mean 'interest in the drama, in a drama, or in dramas (in general)'.[42] Here again, the importance of operating with the true general meaning of a form as opposed to its specific or contextual meanings is clearly evident. The specific meanings of an unmarked category may refer either to the presence in one context or the absence in another of the particular marking in question. One therefore learns nothing about the semantic essence of a form by looking at only certain, even the most commonly occurring, of its contextual usages. Only by studying general meanings can we discover the semantic nature of grammatical morphemes and determine the network of oppositions through which they are structured.

In the Russian case system, the D and A are clearly correlated, respectively, with the I and N as marked terms to corresponding unmarked ones.[43] Whereas the former two cases indicate that the referent is necessarily perceived as the goal of the verbal process (as indirect or direct object respectively), neither the I nor the N provides any information about such a relationship. The negative connotation – that the referent is not the goal of the process – of course occurs in the predominant contextual usages of each of these latter cases, but the positive connotation is not excluded either. Cf. the I usage *oni byli vstrečeny rebenkom* (I) 'They were met by the child (I)', where the I refers to the agent of the process and hence displays no goal-directedness at all, and another I usage *oni vstrečali ego* (A) *rebenkom* (I) 'They met him (A) as a child (I)', where the child is in apposition to the A direct object. Likewise, the chief contextual meaning of the Russian N is to denote the subject of an action – or source of a process as opposed to its goal –, but the N may also have the goal as its referent: cf. passive constructions, where the N is actually the recipient of the action. By the same token, the D and I are correlated with the A and N respectively, in that the former always denote that the phenomenon is marginal to the process, whereas the latter are unmarked in this respect, providing no information about marginal status. In this four-way relationship N–A–I–D, and in fact in the Russian case system as a whole, the N functions as a true *cas zéro*, i.e., as a totally unmarked form. The Russian N does not limit in any way the role of the object it designates; its very lack of meaning in this sense is its general meaning.

Occupying as it does the position of semantically zero case in the Russian case system, the N provides an excellent illustration of the relationships between specific and general meanings within one and the same grammatical form, and an opportunity to study the nature of marking relationships in their true complexity. It would be an oversimplification, for instance, to regard the determination of the general meaning of a form as the only goal of semantic analysis and to view the various specific meanings as merely a mechanical accumulation of contextual applications. In fact we must realize that the question of **general** meanings in a case system is a matter of morphology, an essentially paradigmatic problem, the ultimate goal of which is to establish the network of relations that define the system as a whole. The study of **particular** meanings, however, is equally important for the determination of syntactic relationships and the hierarchy of contextual meanings that results from the syntagmatic application of case forms. If the general meaning of a form is that it is unmarked for a given feature (or set of features) — i.e., that it does not signal either the presence or absence of the feature in question (= non-signalization of x) — , then the **chief** contextual meaning of that form will commonly be that which signals specifically the absence of the particular marking (i.e., signalization of non-x). Each of the cases in Russian other than the N is marked for at least one feature: the range of usage in each is therefore restricted by one or more markings which define a particular kind of relationship between the phenomenon denoted by the noun and the action of the verb. The general meaning of the N, the semantically zero case, is not to signal either the presence or absence of any particular relationship between the noun and the verbal process (i.e., non-signalization of given relationships), and its chief specific meaning is then to signal the absence of any given relationship (i.e., signalization of non-relationship). The principal syntactic usage which corresponds to this signalization of no relationship is that of subject of an action, for the acting subject itself is the source of the process. Of all the contextual usages of the N, this is the chief and also statistically predominant one. The N used alone — i.e., in its pure naming function — of course also has this same basic meaning. Other applications of the N, however, may be interpreted as contextually marked usages with respect to the chief or unmarked ones. The use of the N in passive constructions, for example, is marked with respect to its usage in corresponding active constructions. In a passive construction the referent of the N falls together with that of the A in the corresponding active construction. With the passive, therefore, the N signalizes the presence of x, where x is the marking of the A. Such overlapping in meaning between the N and A represents a contextually marked usage of the unmarked general meaning of the N form.

It must be pointed out, however, that such a marked usage of an unmarked category should not be interpreted as an **extension** of the meaning of the form. Extended meanings are usually identifiable as stylistic variants and ought not to be confused with non-stylistic (non-expressive), purely contextual variations. In stylistic variation there is a metaphorical (or metonymical) connotation present which is perceivable as an additional subjective coloring.[44] In ordinary contextual variation, on the other hand, no such accessory information is present. We can see this clearly in the above examples where the general meaning of the nominative case, being unmarked, already includes the marked usage (presence of x) as one of its logically possible applications. Hence such a usage should not be regarded as an extended meaning, especially when there are no figurative elements present. In distinguishing between contextual and stylistic variations, we may note that "contextual variations point to the concurrent or consecutive neighborhood of the given feature, whereas stylistic variants add a marked — emotive or poetic — annex to the neutral, purely cognitive information of the distinctive feature."[45] Examples of stylistically marked usages are not as common in grammatical meaning as they are in lexical meaning, but they can be found in both domains. A stylistically — as distinct from contextually — marked usage in grammatical meaning occurs when the plural form is used with the meaning of the singular, as, for example, in the polite form of address in French, German, or Russian, or in English when the first person plural replaces the second singular with the addition of an ironic tone, or again in an utterance like: "Someone phoned earlier, but they didn't leave their name." Such genuine extensions of meaning may be viewed as stylistically marked usages of marked forms, the general meaning of the plural being marked with respect to that of the singular.[46] They usually provide a sense of figurative meaning that is not present in the reverse instances where the singular is used with the meaning of the plural, which is simply a contextual variation of the unmarked general meaning of the singular. In the latter case the collective unity of the singular is felt to dominate, leaving no impression of figurativeness or metaphorical usage. It is also significant that the distinction between merely contextual and stylistic variation is normally paralled by the

relatively high statistical frequency of cases of the former as opposed to the latter kind of variation. Examples of contextual
variation where the singular may assume the connotation of more
than one abound in English ('man is mortal' = 'men are mortal',
'they caught their death of cold', 'six head of cattle', 'hundreds
of police', etc.), whereas the occurence of the extended meaning engendered by the use of the plural to refer to an individual
is considerably less common.

When we look at instances where one grammatical category
substitutes for another, it is remarkable the extent to which the
process is one-sided: an unmarked category substitutes for a
corresponding marked category much more frequently than the
other way around. In fact, substitutions in the opposite direction
are relatively rare and normally carry a figurative or stylistic
connotation. This is not to say that the use of an unmarked
form in place of a corresponding marked one is never interpreted
as having figurative meaning: the replacement of either the first
or second person by the unmarked third person may carry an
ironic tone in the former case and a deferential tone in the latter; and the use of the historical present, where the unmarked
present tense substitutes for the marked past tense, is not always
stylistically neutral either. But the obvious predominance of
instances where the unmarked member of a semantically correlated pair of terms replaces the marked member without the
addition of figurative meaning is a direct reflection of the nature
of semantic oppositions. The marked member of a semantic
correlation carries more information than the corresponding
unmarked member, which remains unspecified with respect to
the information in question. Semantic oppositions are thus more
accurately viewed, not as relating a positive to a negative value
or as opposing two polar values but as relating a DEFINITE
term to an INDEFINITE one[47] or a DETERMINATE to an INDE-
TERMINATE term.[48]

A natural consequence of such marking relationships is the
potential for ambiguity which is built into the general meaning
of an unmarked form.[49] All too frequently linguists perceive
semantic ambiguity as evidence for claiming that a form has two

or more "different" meanings, but such a conclusion is often simply the result of a failure to distinguish between general and specific meanings. Thus, for example, one might say that the simple present tense in English has more than one meaning, since it may in different contexts refer to present, past, or future time. In reality, however, it is in the nature of the general meaning of this category that it is temporally unmarked, and this is precisely what produces its potential for ambiguity in the language. The fact that the general meaning of the simple present is unmarked with respect to the other tense categories in English motivates its broad range of usage and explains, for example, why this is the category employed when no specific temporal connotation is implied (e.g. in statements of general truths) or when the specification of temporal relationship is unclear (as when a newspaper headline announces an event which may or may not already have taken place at the time the paper is read). Being unmarked, the simple present in English simply does not give any information about temporal relationship. Such information has to be determined from the context (linguistic or extralinguistic) in which the form appears each time. In contradistinction to the simple present, the other tense forms in English provide more information, and as a consequence the range of contexts in which they can occur tends to be more restricted and their meaning less vague.

It is just this conception of the nature of semantic oppositions that also provides the basis for understanding such relationships as those between polar adjectives and nouns.[50] The adjective 'old' in English is unmarked with respect to 'young'. We ask 'How old is he?' when we don't know whether a person is young or old. If we ask 'How young is he?', than we assume the person is young. Clearly the adjective 'young' carries more information than does 'old'; the former has a more determinate meaning than the latter. The latter is the unmarked term of the opposition and remains vague in meaning. Similarly, 'John is as young as George' tells us that both are young, while 'John is as old as George' leaves the question of their ages open. At the level of the general meaning (Gesamtbedeutung) of such polar adjectives, therefore, we may say that the marked term signals the presence of x, while the unmarked term does not signal either the presence or absence of x. Of course, at the level of the chief contextual meaning (Grundbedeutung) of the unmarked form we may observe specifically the absence of x (or better, signalization of non-x): 'Both John and George are old.' These relationships may be diagrammed, after Holenstein (page 131), as follows:

MARKED TERM   =   Statement of x
UNMARKED TERM   =   (1)   General meaning: non-statement
                                             of x
                               (2)   Specific meaning: statement of
                                             non-x

We may also observe, however, instances where such marking relationships are reversed.[51] In a neutral, purely spatial situation the adjectival phrases 'far from' and 'close to' are in a relationship of unmarked to marked: 'John lives as far from town as George' is less informative than 'John lives as close to town as George'. But in a situation where closeness itself is the norm, a reversal in markedness takes place: 'John is as close (emotionally) to Mary as to Ann' provides less information than 'John is as far (emotionally) from Mary as from Ann'. Here we see the effect of context upon the markings themselves, and the resulting relationships can be explained in terms of semantic COMPATABILITIES: that member of a semantic opposition will be unmarked which conforms more closely to the inherent nature of the concept being expressed. In a spatial context, particularly one of extension, it is the **distance** between two points that best expresses the genus of the category itself, whereas in a relationship of intimacy it is the **closeness** of the parties that is definitive. In each case the neutral or more natural quality, defined with respect to a particular context, will assume the position of the unmarked term.

Such contextually defined reversals of markedness are not at all uncommon. In the Russian case system, for example, the general meaning of the instrumental is marked with respect to that of the nominative, but in specific contexts, these markings too can be reversed. The Russian instrumental (I) is marked, and the nominative (N) unmarked, for the feature of 'marginality': the phenomenon in the I is specified for being peripheral to the narrated situation. In one set of contexts this implies that the object in the I has fleeting or transient qualities. Thus the I is the case normally used as the predicate complement of verbs which denote states of being that do not necessarily last: e.g. *byl studentom* 'was a student', *stal inženerom* 'became an engineer', *ostavalsja spokojnym* 'remained calm', etc. The semantic compatibility between the lexical type of verb and the case of the nominal complement is evident in these examples, and we may conclude that the use of the I here is contextually unmarked, since it remains semantically neutral. When, on the other hand, a predicate nominative is used as the complement of such verbs, the N acquires the specific, contextually marked, connotation of permanent or otherwise special quality: e.g. when a property of an object is specified as inalienable, only the N is possible – *vse oni byli greki* 'They were all Greeks', *mladšij syn byl durak* 'The younger son was a fool'.[52]

Such contextually defined reversals of marking relationships are also common in phonology, where the explanation for them is the same. In vocalic segments compactness is unmarked vs. diffuseness, since it is compactness that represents the optimal vocalic quality. In consonants, on the other hand, diffuseness assumes the position of the unmarked term. As Holenstein notes,

The nature of vowels is predominantly compact, that of consonants diffuse. Vocality and compactness are related features which mutually imply and reinforce each other. Vocalic and diffuse features, on the other hand, clash. Diffuseness encroaches upon vocality. The vowel /u/. . .appears as a non-comforming, exceptional, and differentiated representative of its class.[53]

The phenomenon noted here of "mutual implication and reinforcement", which I have been calling 'compatibility', is of critical importance in linguistic description. Later we shall see the essential role this concept plays in the explanation of syntactic phenomena (Chapter 4). In the present context it is important to underscore the extent to which such linguistic compatibilities define and explain markedness relations in specific contexts at the levels of both sound and meaning, and thereby justify the approach to linguistic invariance being oulined here. One of the major problems in linguistic analysis — indeed one might say the most difficult one — is the establishment of the true invariants in language, a process which implies the ability to identify and explain contextual variations without having recourse to **partial invariance**. Linguists all too frequently stop short of positing real invariants because of the level of abstractness involved and the resulting (sometimes very) broad range of contextual variation that such invariants often encompass. A perfect example of what I am talking about is when a linguist defines semantic invariance on the Grundbedeutung of a given form as opposed to its true invariant meaning, the Gesamtbedeutung. This most frequently happens in the analysis of unmarked forms, where the range of contextual variation is greatest and where, consequently, the relationship of specific meanings to the general meaning is the most difficult to define. We shy away from positing truly abstract invariants in language when we don't have a methodology capable of coming to grips with this problem. Without such a methodology, it is safer simply to define invariance at a less abstract level and thereby reduce the number of apparent counterexamples, at least for the time being.

I make this somewhat harsh and sweeping judgment only because in Jakobson's approach to language I believe we have a methodology adequate to the task. The reason why invariance can be defined at a much more abstract level in this theory is the introduction of the concept of RELATIONAL invariance (see above page 52f), one application of which is to be found in the observation of contextual compatibilities that I have been describing. Without this concept, all the instances of marking reversals we have noted would appear as just so many counterexamples. Once we understand that invariance has to be defined in relative and not in absolute terms, then we can explain the more complicated individual occurrences of a form directly in terms of the invariant feature (or features) we have isolated in the more transparent and straightforward cases. In this way we are not merely describing and classifying surface data, but explaining the occurrence of individual contextual usages in terms of underlying invariant, "material" properties, in sound structure as well as in meaning. This is what explanatory adequacy in linguistics ought to be concerned with.

The concept of relational invariance is probably the most powerful construct in Jakobson's linguistic arsenal, on a par with the notion of rule in generative grammar. It is only through the application of relational or topological invariance, in fact, that we can demonstrate the direct relationship between form and meaning and substantiate the indissoluble nature of the linguistic sign. The determination of the invariant general meaning associated with a given form — that is, the demonstration of the inseparability of a grammatical form and its function — is made feasible only by the realization that those semantic properties that remain unchanged can be defined relative to the effect of an environment (consecutive or concurrent) upon them. What appear on the surface to be disparate usages of the same form, therefore, can be explained as contextual variations upon a single property or set of properties (features). Of course, the invariant conceptual features uncovered will have to be confirmed by a demonstration of their recurrence in other grammatical or lexical categories than the one in which they were originally determined. If this subsequent step can be successfully performed, then we have extremely strong evidence for the reality of the sematic invariants proposed for a given language. To perform this step is to move to the next highest level of invariance in language, which we will call — following C.H. van Schooneveld — intercategorial invariance.[54] To successfully arrive at this stage we must again apply the concept of relational invariance and determine the degree to which the context of a particular grammatical or lexical category (concurrent environment) affects the invariant qualities of a given semantic feature. This is the subject of the next section of this chapter, where we will begin the consideration of van Schooneveld's contribution to this approach.

To conclude the present section, let us note in advance that once the intercategorial invariants have been established for a particular language, we are ready to move to the ultimate level of invariance in language, that of interlingual invariance, or universals. This final step is reached by comparing the intercategorial invariants of several languages. Treated in this manner, the search for semantic universals parallels quite systematically the investigation of phonological universals in Jakobson's approach. The study of semantic universals will be one of the major subjects of the concluding chapter in this book.

4. EXTENSION OF THE ANALYSIS: THE SYSTEM OF RUSSIAN PREPOSITIONS AND PREVERBS

Although it would be odd if a system of such structural elegance as Jakobson has revealed for the Russian cases was not to be found anywhere else in that language, we cannot merely assume that the same features should recur and simply go looking for other manifestations of them. The process of investigation must remain inductive, which means that when we consider another morphological category we must first examine the total range of usage associated with each form to determine the individual invariants of meaning. Only then can the analysis be extended to the next level of invariance where the conceptual properties of one category are compared with those already isolated in another. Rigorous adherence to this methodological requirement has been one of the hallmarks of van Schooneveld's investigation into the semantic structure of morphological categories in Russian, beginning with the study of the sytem of preposition-preverbs and most recently including the analysis of lexical meaning in the Russian verb. In fact, when this research first begun in the early fifties, there was no intention of even looking for confirmation of Jakobson's case features elsewhere in the language. The existence of parallel concepts was discovered in the course of applying the principle of formal determinism to the analysis of Russian prepositions in an entirely independent investigation.

This investigation ultimately yielded a set of five features, three of which turn out to be parallel to the case features. They may be presented as follows:[55]

PREPOSITION/PREVERB SYSTEM		CASE SYSTEM
Dimensionality		
Duplication		
Extension	=	Directionality
Restrictedness	=	Marginality
Objectiveness	=	Quantification

Since we have not yet looked at the nature of any of these features in much detail, I propose that we do so now by concentrating on one of them in a fairly thorough manner – the restrictedness feature as it is realized in the system of Russian prepositions and preverbs – and then consider the relationship of this feature to the marginality feature in the Russian case system. As mentioned before, however, I beg the reader to remember that the data presented here cannot possibly be contrued as representing an exhaustive analysis of a particular preposition or preverb. Whole books have been written on a single Russian preposition, and whatever space is given to a particular form here should be taken as suggestive of its range of contextual application. In selecting examples, however, every effort has been made to consider as broad and heterogeneous a set of contextual variants as possible so as to avoid any implication of felicitousness in the selection process. Classification of the examples is either mine or is common to several standard dictionaries and grammars of Russian.

The two Russian prepositions *ot* and *iz* 'from, out of, etc.' are relatively similar in meaning and therefore provide an obvious place to initiate a discussion of invariant conceptual characteristics. As a preposition, *ot* in a great many of its uses rather transparently denotes the source of the verbal process, whether spacial, temporal, or causal: *ot doma do školy dva kilometra* 'it is two km. *from the house* to the school'; *priem u vrača ot 11 do 3* 'the doctor's office hours are *from 11* to 3'; *polučil pis'mo ot brata* 'received a letter *from (my) brother*'; *imet' detej ot kogo-libo* 'to have children *by someone*'; *trava pogorela ot solnca* 'the lawn was burnt *by the sun*'; *stradat' ot žary* 'to suffer *from the heat*'; *zaprygat' ot radosti* 'jump *for joy*'; *zaviset' ot čego-libo* 'depend *on something*'; etc. The contextual meaning of source of the verbal process needs to be reconciled with a second major variant in the usage of the preposition *ot* — one which, interestingly enough, is also frequently translated by the English 'from' — which includes various senses of maintaining or attaining an abstract distance from something: *zaščiščat' ot solnca* 'protect *from the sun*'; *lekarstvo ot golovnoj boli* 'remedy *for a headache*'; *vozderživat'sja ot golosovanija* 'abstain *from voting*'; etc. To this type clearly belongs the expression *otličat'sja ot (čego-libo)* 'differ *from (something)*'. A third type is represented by such expressions as *ključ ot komnaty* 'key *to the room*', and *pugovica ot pidžaka* 'button *to (from) the jacket*', the essence of which should become clear in a moment.

With these examples in mind let us see if it is not possible to formulate the nature of the semantic link among the three contextual types. What they appear to have in common is that the object of the preposition *ot* denotes a point from which the process either evolves (type 1) or in some respect derives its essence or justification (types 2 and 3). The regimen of this preposition, therefore, acts as the source or orientation point for the verbal process (the narrated situation) — that is, the starting point for the process to take place. In formulating such a common denominator of meaning, all we have to do is unify various senses of the concept of starting point, ranging from the concrete to the abstract. In the first type the point of departure is frequently quite concrete ('from the house to the school', 'from 11 to 3 o'clock'), while in the latter two types it may be abstract to the point of representing, for example, a phenomenon from which the process seeks to remove itself ('a headache remedy' — literally, 'a remedy from a headache'; i.e., a means of leaving a headache behind), or even a phenomenon from which an object derives its essence (as in 'room key' — literally, 'key from (for) a room') where the object of the preposition serves as a reference point for the identification of a particular key.

If we agree that the above formulation fairly accurately characterizes the substantivic (that is, prepositional) function of the morpheme *ot*, let us then consider its application as a verbal prefix, for it is only in the union of the substantival and verbal aspects of the form that we will be able to determine its truly invariant semantic characteristics. A very large number of verbs that take *ot* as a prefix have the meaning of separation from a given point. This meaning is most clearly seen with verbs of motion' *otxodit'* (from *xod* 'go') in different contexts variously assumes connotations of 'leave, withdraw, step aside, deviate from, etc.'. All of these usages suggest a starting point which is left behind by the process. Similarly, *otrjadit'* (from *rjad* 'row') means 'detach'; *otstirat'* means 'wash off'; *otstranit'* 'remove, push aside'; *otnimat'* 'take away, bereave, amputate'; *otryvat'* 'tear off, -away, divert, interrupt; *otklonit'* 'deflect, decline'; *otgovorit'* (from *govor* 'talk') means 'dissuade'; *otvlekat'* 'distract, divert, segregate, abstract'; etc. Within this type we would also want to include verbs where the direction of separation is not to the side, as it were, but behind, as in *otstupit'* 'step back, retreat', *otstat'* 'fall behind', etc.

When we move on to other examples where the concept of separation from a point is not so transparent, it is evident that the conceptual unity of the form will have to be formulated in somewhat different, more abstract terms. Another sub-category of the usage of *ot* as a preverb, for example, has the meaning of reversing a process, and frequently coincides with English *re-* in this sense: *otdat'* 'return' (from *dat'* 'give'); *otplatit'* 'repay'; *otvetit'* 'reply' (from *vet* 'say, speak'); *otkazat'* 'refuse' (from *kaz* 'state'); *otrazit'* 'reflect' (from *raz* 'strike'); etc. Obviously related to this type are such verbs as *otvintit'* 'remove, unscrew' (from *vint* 'screw') *otkryt'* 'open, uncover' (from *kroj* 'cover'), and another set of verbs which has the meaning of undoing a process: *otkrepit'* 'unfasten' (from *krep* 'strong'); *otstegnut'* 'unfasten' (from *steg* 'stitch, button'); *otkuporit'* 'uncork'; *otprjagat'* 'unharness'; etc. The easiest way to describe what is common to this second type, which implies reversing or undoing a process, is to consider the effect the preverb has upon the meaning of the lexical root to which it is attached. In all cases it appears that the preverb presupposes the lexical meaning of the verbal root and then operates semantically upon the lexical morpheme in a specific way; to wit, specifies the perspective that the lexical meaning of the verb will assume at least once the verbal process has been completed.[56] In verbs denoting reversal of the process, the lexical meaning of the verb is reversed by the operation of the prefix *ot* upon it, so that at the end of the process the particular lexical meaning is cancelled and the reverse situation is in effect. Thus *otplatit'* implies cancellation of a 'paying' situation such that by performing the process an individual will be paid back; *otvetit'* means to cancel a 'speaking' situation – that is, to return speech by answering; *otkryt'* means to cancel a 'cover' situation, hence 'open'; and so forth. The verbs of undoing can obviously be treated in the same manner: *otkryt'*, for example, means both 'open' and 'uncover', denoting in either case cancellation of a 'cover' situation.

It is extremely important to note at this point, however, that what we are defining here when we speak of undoing a process is not just any situation that might correspond to English *un-*, but a specific type of 'un-' situation that implies cancellation of a process and is systematically identified in Russian by the use of the preverb *ot*. There are, in fact, several different types of 'un-' situations, each of which is correlated with a different formal property in the Russian language. Thus, for example, by far the most common type is that which denotes mere negation and systematically corresponds to Russian *ne-*. Another common type specifically denotes breaking up of a unity, and this type regularly occurs in Russian with the preverb *raz* (~ *ras*): *razvjazat'* 'untie', *razgruzat'* 'unload', *raspakovat'* 'unpack', etc. There is no question that such conceptual distinctions as these are central to the semantic structure of Russian, whereas they are not in English to the extent that they all correspond to the single formal property *un-*. In English for example, we do not differentiate formally between untying a knot and untying a horse, but in Russian there is a systematic formal and conceptual distinction between the two: the former involves unravelling a unity and the verb used is *razvjazat'*; the latter concerns rather the operation of releasing the horse — that is, cancelling a 'tied up' situation — and the verb used is *otvjazat'*. What makes these distinctions central to the semantic structure of Russian is that the differences in form are systematically correlated with conceptual oppositions that permeate the entire grammatical and lexical stock of the language. In other words, the conceptual invariant that is needed to exlain why *otvjazat'* is used in the expression 'untie a horse' but not in the case of 'untie a knot' is just the one that explains the use of *ot* in the meaning of reversing a process and, as I am about to demonstrate, also in the sense of separation from a point. Ultimately, as we shall see, the invariant associated with *ot* as both preposition and preverb is also common to a number of other preposition-preverbs and correlates as well with Jakobson's feature of marginality in the Russian case system,. . .and so forth, even into the structure of the verbal lexicon.

Looking back now at the first subtype of prefixal *ot*, we may formulate the concept of separation from a point in terms of the same cancellation operation that was evidenced in verbs of reversing or undoing a process. Only this time it is not so much the process itself that is cancelled as it is the relation between some object and an initial reference point that is terminated by virtue of performing the verbal process, rather more like the uses of *ot* as a preposition. When the verb is transitive, it is the relationship between the direct object and the reference point that is cancelled: thus *otgovorit'* 'dissuade' means to speak in such a way that the relation between the object (person) and some idea, thought, or whatever will be cancelled; *otnimat'* 'take away, etc.' means to take in such a way that the object of the taking will be separated from some point; and so forth. When, on the other hand, the verb is intransitive, it is the relation between the subject and the starting point that is cancelled: in *otstupat'* 'step back, retreat' the subject's relation to the initial point is terminated by the process, as it is in *otstat'* 'fall behind'.

Several considerations suggest that we do indeed have to do here with contextual variations of one and the same invariant cancellation operation. For one thing, in many cases the choice of which subtype of cancellation, the reversal or the separation type, we assign a verb to is quite arbitrary. Does *otkryt'* 'open' mean to reverse a cover situation or to move a cover aside? Does *otprjagat'* 'unharness' mean to reverse a harness situation or to take a harness off? Evidently for Russian in such cases the question is moot because the difference is not distinctive. Another consideration is that the same verb may have one or the other connotation in different contexts: *otdat'* can variously mean 'return' or 'give up or away', as in *otdat' zamuž* 'give (away) in marriage', *otdat' pod stražu* 'give into custody', or even *otdat' jakor'* 'drop anchor'. I included *otrazit'* 'reflect' under the reversal type above, having in mind a visual return, but this verb is also used in the sense of 'ward off, repel, etc.', suggesting rather a separation situation. And finally, in many (though certainly not all) cases, the reversal types, even when transitive in English, tend not to take accusative direct objects in Russian, whereas the separation types do, which suggests that the distinction is at least partly distributional. Instead of accusatives we find dative objects with *otvetit' komu* 'answer someone' (cf. *otgovorit' kogo* [acc.] dissuade someone', where the accusative occurs with an almost identical root morpheme) and *otplatit' komu* 'repay someone'; and/or we find prepositional complements, as in *otvetit' na vopros* 'answer a question' or *otkazat' v čem* 'refuse something'.

It appears, then, that we do have an invariant here, which may be defined as cancellation or termination of a situation that is in effect at the onset of the verbal process, by virtue of performing the verbal process. In other words, in all the uses of *ot* described so far, there is an initial situation the validity of which is necessarily restricted to the particular narrated event, since completion of the verbal process (i.e., culmination of the narrated event) brings about the termination of that situation. This, in van Schooneveld's terminology, is the feature of **restrictedness.**[57] In the prepositional uses of *ot* there is an initial situation (or point) that is necessarily left behind by the process.[58] And the same holds true, as we have just seen, for the prefixal uses of *ot*, of which there is yet one more type to consider. I have left this third type until last because I think it illustrates quite graphically the essence of the restrictedness feature. In this third type the prefix *ot* denotes completion of the process, but not just any type of completion, for there are several different types in Russian, just as there are various types of undoing a process, each signified by a different verbal prefix. The prefix *po*, for example, usually denotes completion by doing a little bit of something (*porabotat'* 'do some, a bit of work', *pomaxat'* 'give a wave, wave for a while', *pokurit'* 'have a smoke', *posidet'* 'sit for a while', etc.). The prefix *iz* also denotes completion, but in the sense of doing to exhaustion (*izbit'* 'beat unmercifully', *ispol'-zovat'* 'use up', *iznosit'* 'wear out (clothes)', *izrisovat'* 'scribble all over, cover the paper', etc.). To appreciate the sense of finishing that is imparted by the prefix *ot*, let us look at an extended list of examples. *Otbyt'* (from *byt'* 'be') means to 'serve time'; *otslužit'* (from *služit'* 'serve') also means to 'serve time', or it can mean 'be worn out'; *otžit'* (from *žit'* 'live') means 'become obsolete'; *otdelat'* (from *delat'* 'do') means 'put on the finishing touches, trim'; *otrabotat'* (from *rabotat'* 'work') means 'work off, clear by working'; *otmyt'* (from *myt'* 'wash') means 'wash off, wash clean'; *otpit'* (from *pit'* 'drink') means 'take a sip'; and finally, there is a whole series of verbs which simply mean to finish a process: *otpoit'* 'finish watering', *otpljasat'* 'finish dancing', *otužinat'* 'finish supper', *otcvesti* 'to cease blooming', etc. It is clear from these examples that *ot* does not mean to finish once and for all. The sense of completion that is imparted by *ot* is not absolute, but rather seems to be limited to a particular application of the process denoted by the lexical meaning of the verb. When the verbal process is itself of a concrete nature, as it is in the last set of examples, then the addition of *ot* merely implies termination of the process involved. But where the lexical meanings are of a more general nature, the addition of *ot* implies termination of a specific instance of that process: *otpit'* 'take a sip' means to complete one instance of a drinking situation; *otmyt'* 'wash clean' means to finish one washing operation;

otrabotat' means to finish a particular job, as does *otdelat'* 'to apply finishing touches'. The most revealing examples are those where the lexical meaning of the verb denotes a span of time rather than performance of an action. Here it is quite obvious that *ot* means to complete performing the process only as far as the given narrated situation is concerned: *otbyt'* 'serve time' means to stop being with reference to a specific situation; *otslužit'* is interesting because it combines two senses of cancelling a specific serving situation − to 'serve time' as above and to 'be worn out', that is, to cease to be of service in a given situation; *otžit'* means to 'become obsolete', that is, to cease to have life with respect to a particular situation. All that this type of completion says, then, is that the validity of the verbal lexical meaning (denoted by the root morpheme) is restricted to the given narrated situation.

This kind of cancellation illustrates the restrictedness feature par excellence, as we have defined it herein. Ultimately we may have to modify somewhat our perception of how restrictedness operates in the preposition-preverb *ot* because, in addition to being marked for restrictedness, *ot* is apparently also marked for a second feature, extension (cf. Jakobson's directionality).[59] The union of these two features produces certain peculiarities consideration of which lies beyond the scope of the present discussion, except to say that it is evidently this second feature that explains why, in *ot*, the starting point, even though it is left behind by the process, still seems to remain as a reference point during the process (cf. especially *ključ ot komnaty* 'room key'). By contrast, in the preverb *pere-*, for example, which we will consider below, the feature of restrictedness is present without extension, and the starting point no longer remains as a reference point for the process. Before considering *pere-*, however, let us turn to the preposition-preverb *iz* which, because of its greater similarity to *ot*, will provide us a slightly better picture of the application of the restrictedness feature.

There is no doubt that the prepositional uses of *iz* clearly involve cancellation of a relationship to a starting point. In fact, this aspect of the meaning of *iz* as a preposition is so transparent that one might wonder why we did not begin this exposition of restrictedness with *iz* instead of *ot*. The reason is simply that the range of contextual application of the preposition *iz* is so relatively circumscribed that one immediately suspects that much more than one feature must by involved. Generally speaking, the narrower the range of usage of a form, the more highly marked it is. And in fact, as we shall see, this is the case with *iz*.

The prepositional uses of *iz* are commonly subdivided into roughly the following categories: (1) place from which the process originates: *priexal iz goroda* 'came from town'; (2) source of the process: *uznal iz gazety* 'found out from the newspaper', *čelovek iz rabočej sem'i* 'person from a working family'; (3) material out of which something is made: *dom iz dereva* 'house made of wood'; (4) a whole from which a part derives: *nekotorye iz studentov* 'several of the students'; (5) causal source: *sdelat' iz ljubvi* 'do out of love'. Obviously the feature of restrictedness is present in all of these types. What distinguishes the uses of *iz* as a preposition from those of *ot* appears to have something to do with the nature of the source itself. Rather than being merely a point as it is frequently with *ot*, the source of the process from which *iz* originates is always more complex: it has a structure of its own, so to speak; it is, as van Schooneveld suggests, dimensional.[60] The difference between *iz* and *ot* in this respect can be seen most clearly in minimal pairs such as *vyšel iz doma* 'came out of the house' vs. *otošel ot doma* 'moved away from the house'. When the process emanates from inside of a dimensional source, *iz* must be used, whereas *ot* occurs when the source is merely perceived as a reference point. Likewise, one says *uznal iz gazety* 'found out from the newspaper', but *uznal ot nego* 'found out from him': in general in Russian, when persons are involved, the source of the process is seen as a point, unless the process physically emanates from the person's insides, in which case the source assumes dimensions and the preposition *iz* can occur. With objects that are relatively concrete, this distinction is rather easy to see. As, however, the nature of the source becomes more abstract, the two types seem to become almost interchangeable. One finds *drožat' ot straxa* 'shake from (with) fear' alongside *sdelat' iz straxa* 'do out of fear'. It is possible in such cases that when the fear is the source of some conscious action on the part of the subject it is perceived as dimensional, but when the activity is involuntary, a point. If this analysis is correct, then we may say that the difference between these two prepositions is expressible in terms of a feature which we will call **dimensionality**: *iz* is marked for dimensionality whereas *ot* is unmarked. Both prepositions are marked for restrictedness.[61]

The various preverbial uses of *iz* (~ *is*) also demonstrate that this form is definitely marked for restrictedness. We have already encountered one of them in our discussion of types of completion above – *iz* as a preverb imparts the meaning of carrying out a process to an extreme or to exhaustion: cf. *ispisat'* 'use up by writing (pencil or paper)' (from *pisat'* 'write'); *izbit'* 'beat unmercifully'; etc: (See above, page 86.) Once again, the meaning of completion – that is, cancellation of the process by virtue of its being performed in the given narrated situation – is imparted by the restrictedness feature, as it was in *ot*, but this time the additional connotation of maximal fullness or exhaustion of the process further qualifies the nature of the cancellation operation. This evidently is the result of the union of restrictedness with dimensionality again, a fact which I will merely state at this point, with the understanding that we will return to a discussion of maximal fullness of the process as a contextual variant of dimensionality very shortly, when we consider the meaning of the perfective aspect in Russian. For the moment let me simply add that the difference in types of completion represented by restrictedness alone on the one hand and restrictedness combined with dimensionality on the other reminds one very much of the distinction in English evident in the expression , 'It may be over between us, but it's not finished.'[62]

Another type of the use of *iz* as a verbal prefix parallels quite closely the prepositional use of the form in the sense of direction out from a dimensional source, as in *isxodit'* (from *xodit'* 'go') which variously means 'come, issue, originate, proceed, -from'. Cf. *otxodit'* 'leave, withdraw, step aside, deviate from' (above, page 82), where the source is clearly not dimensional. The verb *isxodit'*, incidentally, includes as possible meanings virtually all of the contextual types of *iz* noted so far, demonstrating once again the extent to which we are dealing with contextual variants of a single invariant set of conceptual characteristics. Not only does *isxodit'* mean 'come from, etc.', but in other contexts it may mean 'walk or stroll all over' (colloquial) or, in certain fixed expressions, 'bleed to death' (*isxodit' krov'ju* — literally '(completely) come out from with blood'), or 'cry one's heart out' (*isxodit' slezami* — literally '(completely) come out from with tears'). The variant meaning of completion to exhaustion is obvious here, as is the connotation of maximal fullness of the process in the deverbal form *isxod* 'outcome, result, end', which occurs in such expressions as *na isxode dnja* 'at the end of the day'. Other examples of *iz* which clearly derive from the meaning of 'out from' include *izbežat'* 'avoid, evade, steer clear of, escape' (literally 'run from'; cf. *otbežat'* which means 'run off, to the side', where the source of the running is merely a point and does not have nearly the significance (dimensions) that is (are) present in the source of *izbežat'*); *izdat'* 'publish, issue (an order), utter (a sound), exhale (a breath)' — literally 'give out from'; *ispolnit'* 'carry out, execute, fulfill', where once again the meanings of 'out' and completion to maximal fullness come together in a single form; and *izbrat'* 'elect, choose' — literally 'take from'.

To further illustrate the scope of restrictedness in the system of Russian verbal prefixes, let us consider very briefly two additional forms: *vy-* and *pere-*. I say briefly because I propose to demonstrate only the presence of the restrictedness feature at this time and not consider the relationship of these two preverbs to each other or to *ot* and *iz*, since to do so would necessitate a lengthy treatment of other features which is not central to the present discussion. The relationship among all four forms is presented graphically below (page 103) and is discussed in detail in van Schooneveld's *Semantic Transmutations* (pp. 125ff). At this point I merely want to present some additional contextual applications of the restrictedness feature as it occurs in the Russian preverbial system, after which we will return to the case system for a comparative analysis of restrictedness and its case system counterpart, marginality.

Neither *vy-* nor *pere-* occurs as a preposition, only as a preverb, a fact for which van Schooneveld offers an explanation based upon the total feature composition of these two forms as compared with *ot* and *iz*.[63] As a preverb, *vy-* is nearly identical in meaning to *iz*, and therefore presents no difficulty in identifying the presence of restrictedness. Like *iz*, *vy-* may impart the meaning of out from a dimensional source, as in *vyxodit' iz doma* 'leave the house' (where it frequently occurs in conjunction with the preposition *iz*); *vyvodit'* 'lead out, deduce'; *vypisat'* 'write out, extract'; etc. The major type of preverbial *vy-* again has the meaning of completion, but with slightly different overtones than were present in either *ot* or *iz*: *vyigrat'* 'win' (literally 'play out'); *vydumat'* 'invent' (literally 'think out'); *vyučit'* 'learn by heart' (literally 'study out'); or simply *vypit'* 'drink up'; *vykurit'* 'finish smoking'; etc. How to characterize the particular kind of completion that is represented by *vy-* is, as I have suggested, beyond the scope of this discussion, but there is no doubt that we have to do here once again with some form of restrictedness.

Before proceeding to the analysis of the fourth preverb, *pere-*, some additional remarks are in order regarding the concept of completion. We have been observing several different types of completion here, and have claimed that common to all of them so far is the feature of restrictedness. Since, as any Slavist knows, the Russian verb also has an aspect system where the perfective form of the verb (as opposed to the imperfective) most frequently imparts the meaning of completion of the action, it is natural to assume that restrictedness might also be the mark of the perfective aspect. In fact, however, such a conclusion turns out to be unwarranted, and a brief demonstration of this fact at this point will allow us to reexamine some very important methodological considerations vital to the discussions that follow.

To get right to the point regarding aspect in Russian we may note that the perfective, though it most frequently does signalize completion of the action, is not by any means limited to this one meaning. Completion may be the Grundbedeutung of the perfective aspect, but it is not the Gesamtbedeutung. To isolate the true general meaning of the category we have to consider its other contextual applications which, inter alia, include its use as a future tense (in Russian, present perfective = future) as well as its occurrence when one action does not begin until another has ended (in which case both processes are usually expressed by perfective verbs): e.g. 'he crossed the room and sat down'. In each of these latter two types it is the starting point as well as the end point of the process that is involved. Future time implies and absolute initial limit to the process that is posterior to the moment of speaking, which we may diagram thus:

speech event   narrated event: future
(moment of speaking)   (verbal process)

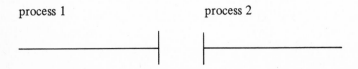

By the same token, a sequence of actions implies a similar relationship between two verbal processes:

process 1   process 2

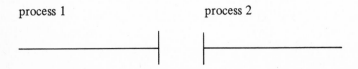

In each of these cases there is focus on the initial limits of the process, whereas in the meaning of completion, the focus is on the final limits. Putting these contextual types together we may say that the perfective gives outlines or dimensions to the process in one or the other respect, its beginning or its end. And we may diagram the invariant of meaning thus:

The perfective, therefore, presents a process as having dimensions, whereas the imperfective doesn't stipulate whether there are dimensions or not. In van Schooneveld's terminology the perfective is marked, and the imperfective unmarked, for **dimensionality**.[64]

The notion of completion as it occurs in the perfective aspect, therefore, is a contextual variant of dimensionality rather than restrictedness, a conclusion which should not surprise us at all if we think back for a moment to the different types of completion signalized by *iz* vs. *ot*. The difference between *iz* and *ot*, we have noted, has to do with whether or not the type of completion entails maximal fullness of the process. In *iz* it did, and we suggested that this form was additionally marked for dimensionality. In *iz* the concept of completion as such is a form of cancellation, which is given by the restrictedness feature, while dimensionality gives only the connotation of maximal fullness. By contrast, the perfective aspect, which is marked for dimensionality and unmarked for restrictedness, has as its invariant characteristic the concept of maximal fullness; i.e., focus on the limits of the process. Which limit is focused upon, the beginning or the end, is a contextual variation of the fact that the process has dimensions. In other words, the perfective aspect does not signalize a cancellation operation, but rather the dimensionality of the process. To the extent that the dimension focused upon in a given context is the final as opposed to the initial limit of the process, we will perceive an overlap in meaning with the concept of cancellation, just as we perceive an overlap in meaning with active and passive constructions. In both cases the methodological principle that must be kept in mind is that semantic features are defined on general meanings; i.e., as an invariant function of a given formal category in all of its contextual applications. We will return to the semantics of aspect in Russian in Chapter 5.

Consider now the preverb *pere-*, which does not have completion as one of its contextual variants, but does, we would have to conclude, have other connotations that fall within the characteristics defined by restrictedness. In fact, *pere-* represents pure restrictedness, uncomplicated by any further semantic colorings. In its purest form, restrictedness merely denotes a situation that is left behind by the verbal process — that is, a situation that is cancelled by virtue of performing the process. One of the major contextual usages of *pere-* has the meaning 'across, through, over': e.g. *perexodit'* 'cross over, shift' (from *xodit'* 'go'); *perevodit'* 'transfer, translate' (from *vodit'* 'lead'); *perestupit'* 'step across' (from *stupit'* 'step'); *peredat'* 'hand over, pass' (from *dat'* 'give'); *perežit'* 'survive, experience' (literally 'live through'); *perenočevat'* 'stay overnight'; and *peregoret'* 'burn out (through)'. The last three examples are very reminiscent of preverbial types of completion we have already seen, and strongly suggest a conceptual link between the two operations 'through, over, across' and cancellation. In both instances, and in all the examples above, there is a situation that is left behind by the process. Further evidence for this conceptual link can be found in the use of English 'over' in the same two senses, which we have already noted (see note 62 at end of chapter) and which we see here again in 'hand over' vs. 'stay overnight'. Of still further interest is the fact that there are even more senses of English 'over' which coincide with Russian *pere-*, namely that of doing to excess, as in *pereplatit'* 'overpay', *pereocenit'* 'overestimate', etc.; and that of repeating a process (or doing something 'over'), as in *perepisat'* 'rewrite' or 'write over again', *peredelat'* 'redo', etc. Closely related to repetition of a process are several subtypes in which the preverb *pere-* occurs, including (1) reciprocal action (i.e., repeating a process by performing it back and forth), as in *perepisyvat'sja* 'correspond' (from *pisat'* 'write') and *peregovaryvat'sja* 'exchange talk with' (from *govorit'* 'talk'); and (2) completion through repeated performance, as in *perelovit'* 'catch all of, one at a time' and *perestreljat'* 'shoot all of, one at a time', etc. To repeat a process and to overcomplete it both necessarily imply that the process has been cancelled (that is, minimally finished) already once in the situaton described.

    In this same context we should recall that the English *re-*, which occurs here in the sense of performing a process over again, also occurred in another major variant of restrictedness, that of reversing a process, which we observed in connection with the preverb *ot* above. Such coincidences of formal and semantic properties as are evident in the cases of both *over* and *re-* are hardly accidental and suggest strong conceptual affinities of a fairly abstract nature across languages. A conceptual property something like restrictedness, in other words, probably exists in different languages, at least in the Indoeuropean family, but its exact identity in each language would have to be determined individually through language-specific analyses of observable formal properties, for the coincidences we observe may be instructive, and certainly can be used as evidence for conceptual affinity, but they should not be mistaken for semantic identity between languages, or be treated as universals per se. To appreciate this fact, all we have to do is consider the English *over*, which has contextual applications that can never occur with the Russian *pere-*, namely in the static spatial meaning of 'above' (as in 'the lamp hung over the table'), or in any strictly prepositional usage, since the Russian *pere-* does not occur as a preposition. How one approaches the study of universals from the perspective of sign theory as outlined here will be a subject for consideration in the final chapter.

Now that we have observed a fairly heterogeneous set of specific applications of the restrictedness feature as it occurs in the system of Russian prepositions and preverbs, we are in a position to return to the Russian case system and consider how the concept of restrictedness relates to the case feature marginality. In the previous section we noted that the instrumental case in Russian is marked for only the one feature marginality, and I propose to use this case to exemplify the concept of marginality in its most uncomplicated form. Let us look first at some examples we have already seen. In the discussion of semantic compatibilities above (pages 75-6), we observed that the instrumental normally occurs as the predicate complement of verbs that denote states of being that do not necessarily last, as in *byl studentom* 'was a student', *stal inženerom* 'became an engineer', or *ostavalsja spokojnym* 'remained calm'. We remarked at the time that the instrumental in such instances suggests that the predicate complement has fleeting or transient properties that distinguish this type of construction from an otherwise identical one using a predicate nominative, in which case the predicate tends to assume the status of inalienable or otherwise permanent quality. With the benefit of our subsequent consideration of restrictedness we may now qualify this statement and propose that what the feature of marginality really denotes in such instances is a quality that is not necessarily valid beyond its occurrence in the given narrated event. In other words, the instrumental poses the question of the potential cancellation of a phenomenon's applicability outside the given narrated situation — that is, specifies that the validity of the phenomenon in the predicate is potentially, if not actually, restricted to its occurrence in the particular narrated event. The concept of restrictedness is really quite transparent in this type of usage and, I trust, does not require further elaboration. In other types, however, the equivalence of marginality and restrictedness is not so transparent and therefore needs to be discussed in greater detail.

In his 1936 and 1958 formulations Jakobson defined marginality as denoting a phenomenon that is peripheral to the situation described (narrated event). Hence the term marginality. In this formulation the instrumental case is said to signal that a phenomenon serves only as an accompanying circumstance or mere instrument of the verbal process — as opposed to its being, for example, the goal or focus of the process, which is the mark of the accusative case. Thus in the examples involving verbs of 'using' discussed above (pages 64ff) we observed that the instrumental occurs when the object that is being used is less directly involved in the verbal process. Stated in this way, however, the concept of marginal circumstance or mere instrument is rather difficult to reconcile with the feature of restrictedness because when the case usages are presented in this manner, the definitions of marginality and restrictedness are being formulated at entirely different levels. We are, as it were, trying to compare apples and oranges. What we need to do is find a common linguistic ground upon which to base both case-type relations and the sort of properties we observed in the Russian prepositions and preverbs. The first set of examples involving the instrumental above did not present so much of a problem in this respect because, though we were dealing with case relations, we were nevertheless operating with verbal (that is, quasi-temporal) concepts – in this instance verbs that denote states of being that do not necessarily last. If we can transpose the essence of marginality into a similarly quasi-temporal formulation, then we will have established some sort of common semantic ground.

To accomplish this task, what we have to do is to reorient our perspective vis-à-vis marginal or peripheral status, which is most easily done by first comparing what is marginal to what is central in an utterance. In the "Beitrag zur allgemeinen Kasuslehre" Jakobson made note of the fact that if we take a transitive verb such as *delat'* 'do' in Russian, the minimal utterance one can construct using this verb will have to provide at least two pieces of information: information about 'who did' and about 'did what'. In other words, the minimal utterance involving a transitive verb presupposes at least a subject and a direct object. If either of these elements is not syntactically expressed, it will still be implied because these two elements, which are represented by the nominative and accusative cases repectively in Russian, are both central to the meaning of the process. Other possible information, such as the answer to any of the questions 'how', 'with (or by means of) what', 'why', etc., is clearly secondary and its absence not felt as critical. The uses of the instrumental case in Russian obviously fall into this latter category of secondary or peripheral information.

With this distinction between central and peripheral phenomena in mind we can now pose the very basic question of what it is an utterance does; i.e., what is it we accomplish when we speak? Obviously, speaking allows us to communicate, but it does so by the speaker creating a set of relationships for the addressee to perceive something. If in the set of linguistic relationships that constitutes an utterance, some elements are more central than others, it stands to reason that these more central elements will be the ones that, as far as the addressee is concerned, remain in focus once the utterance has been completed. (Obviously we are not talking here about a specific hearer's conscious perception of the relative impact of different linguistic elements, but about an abstract addressee employing his subconscious linguistic competence.) To illustrate this point, consider the Russian accusative case, which clearly functions as the central goal or focus of an utterance. If one says *ja napisal stat'ju* 'I wrote an article (acc.)', the set of relationships established by this utterance actually creates, from the linguistic point of view, the article. The article becomes for the addressee an element brought into being, as it were, by the process and its effects therefore remain in force beyond the narrated event itself.[65] Even in such an utterance as *ja pročital stat'ju* 'I read the article (acc.)', where the direct object does not in any physical sense come into being, the status of the phenomenon in the accusative actually does change for the addressee, since the article becomes a 'read' article by virtue of the linguistic situation presented. When, therefore, a phenomenon is given as central or focal by the linguistic process, we may say that its effects remain valid beyond the narrated event itself – that is, in a quasi-temporal sense, valid in a situation posterior to that of the narrated event, which we may assume for the purposes of this discussion is the situation in which the addressee participates as recipient of the message being transmitted. Hence van Schooneveld's renaming of Jakobson's directionality feature as **extension**: the status of the phenomenon remains valid beyond the narrated event.

By contrast, a phenomenon presented as marginal in the narrated event is one which, from the point of view of the posterior addressee, does not retain its validity beyond the narrated situation itself. As far as the addressee is concerned, a marginal element is one which is always at least potentially replaceable by another phenomenon once the situation described in the narrated event has been expressed. Viewed from this perspective, marginality indeed does equate with restrictedness. Consider, for example, the use of the instrumental case in the Russian expression *govorit' rezkimi slovami* 'speak in a harsh tone' (literally 'speak with harsh words [inst.]'). Here the words act as a manner adverbial which merely qualifies the way the speaking takes place in the given narrated situation; the focal point of the utterance remains the act of speaking itself. By contrast, in *govorit' rezkie slova* 'to utter sharp words [acc.]' the focus of the narrated situation shifts to the object and the addressee perceives, as it were, the words produced by the process. In the first example the emphasis is on the process itself, in the second on what the process produces. Such doublets are, as Jakobson notes, not merely stylistic synonyms, but are formally distinct utterances which consistently maintain the opposition between peripheral and central phenomena, in this case "between the medium and the goal, between the implement and the self-sufficient object," each of which, I am suggesting, is perceived differently by the addressee.[66]

By reformulating Jakobson's case features in this manner, we are merely transposing a set of definitions based upon observation of the inner workings of the narrated event alone (directionality, marginality, etc.) into a set defined rather on the relationship between elements of the narrated situation and their effect upon the addressee as observer of the outcome of the narrated event -- as recipient of the message. Since, of course, the speaker himself is also ultimately his own addressee, we may alter our terminology somewhat and refer instead to the speech situation in general as the posterior situation from the perspective of which the case features are identified, without altering any essential elements of our definitions. By proceeding in this manner we have succeeded in determining a common ground upon which to make meaningful comparisons of features isolated in different morphological categories, which is one of the major achievements of van Schooneveld's approach. This achievement is all the more significant in that it allows us to remove much of the impressionistic character of the feature specifications by applying a consistent measure to their definition -- a critical consideration if the features we are operating with are to be objectively verifiable.

I shall return to the issue of verifiability in Chapter 5. At this point I think it would be instructive to present in at least graphic form the structure of the Russian preposition-preverb system as it has been worked out to date by van Schooneveld.[67] Here once

more we see a semantic system of unusual structural elegance arrived at by the consistent examination of invariant paradigmatic
relations. In the diagram that follows the morphemes are again
presented in the graphic form of cubes, adding a new dimension
each time we add a new feature. The features are those given at
the beginning of this section: dimensionality, duplication, extension, restrictedness, and objectiveness. To represent these five
features we might construct a five-dimensional cube, but to do
so would significantly reduce the visual clarity we are trying to
achieve. We can instead add additional dimensions simply by
adding cubes in the same order that lines were added to construct the original cube of three dimensions. Thus, if the first
feature is represented by a line upwards from the starting point
to create two points, the top marked and the bottom unmarked,
a fourth feature can be added in the same manner by construct-
ing a cube above the original cube, where the entire cube would
be marked and the bottom one unmarked for this feature, and
so forth. Thus the following order obtains:

Feature 1: Dimensionality
            (line)

Feature 2: Duplication
            (square)

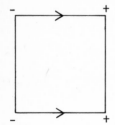

Feature 3: Extension
           (cube)

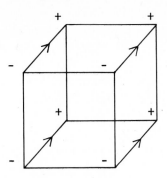

Feature 4: Restrictedness
           (line of cubes)

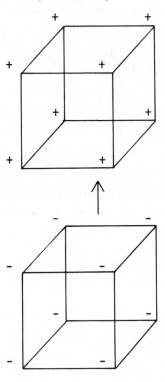

Feature 5: Objectiveness
          (square of cubes)

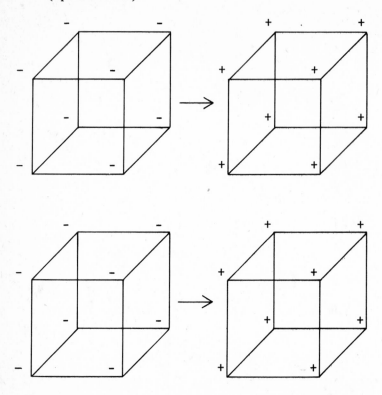

Each time a new feature is added the number of vertexes at which possible preposition-preverbs are located doubles, while the relationships among the forms within each individual cube remain the same.

The system of Russian preposition-preverbs may be represented as follows:

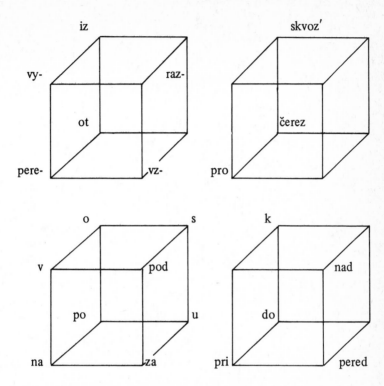

As one might imagine from the discussion of the four forms *pere-*, *vy-*, *ot*, and *iz* above, it is virtually impossible to provide meaningful English glosses for each form in a way that would accurately represent their ranges of usage, especially as preverbs. Nevertheless, the following list is given with the understanding that only the basic prepositional uses of each form are accounted for, and even these may be misleading when presented out of context. Forms that occur only as preverbs are marked as bound morphemes (followed by a dash).

na	'on, at, onto, to'
v	'in, into, to'
za	'behind, beyond, in exchange for'
pod	'under'

po	'along, according to'
o	'about, concerning, against'
u	'at, near, by'
s	'with, (down) from, off of'

pere-	'across, over; re-'
vy-	'out; up' (as in 'finish up')
ot	'(away) from'
iz	'out of, from'
vz-	'up' (as in 'bring up'); 're-'
raz-	'un-'; etc.

pri	'associated with, in the presence of, -time of'
do	'until, before, as far as'
k	'to, toward'
pered	'before, in front of'
nad	'over, above'

pro	'about'
čerez	'through (time or space)'
skvoz'	'across, through'

The comparative study of the features themselves as abstract semantic concepts is a subject of major importance for the valuable insights it provides into the nature of the peculiarly linguistic logic that lies behind such a set of concepts. We will address this subject later (in Chapter 5) once we have observed the application of more of the features in specific morphological categories. For now, let us turn to the analysis of lexical meaning to gain some further understanding of the role such features play in different morphological settings.

5. TRANSITION TO LEXICAL MEANING

When we proceed from grammatical to lexical meaning it is evident that even five features will not suffice to account for the variety of conceptual types encountered, for the maximum number of distinctions a five-feature binary system can handle is 32. The question of what types of features are necessary to describe lexical categories is a complicated one that can only be addressed by examining the formal data and observing the kinds of conceptual oppositions that are displayed there. This requires making the rather crucial decision of what data to look at first, a task which is complicated by the fact that in lexical as opposed to grammatical meaning we are dealing with open-ended categories. A logical way to proceed in this matter would be to determine which lexical categories are likely to reveal conceptual properties that lend themselves most readily to definition in terms similar to those encountered in the realm of grammatical meaning. Such a procedure is dictated not so much by the expectation of finding the same features back again in lexical categories — though this certainly remains a strong possibility not to be ignored — but rather by the practical consideration that we have now determined a common ground upon which to base feature definitions that greatly facilitates the definition process, and to be in a position to build upon the groundwork already laid simply makes good sense. In analyzing grammatical meaning we evolved a framework for defining conceptual categories based upon viewing a given phenomenon always in the dual perspective of how it relates to the narrated event in which it occurs on the one hand and how it appears to an observer of the ensuing speech situation on the other. Since defining grammatical categories in these terms proved to be so consistently productive, we can conclude that the two sets represented by the narrated event and the speech event are in fact semantic primitives, at least within the realm of grammatical meaning. From a more purely heuristic point of view, one of the reasons this approach worked so well is that we were able to gain a greater degree of objectivity in defining abstract conceptual properties by formulating them in quasi-temporal terms. If we now turn to the realm of lexical meaning with this consideration in mind, it would seem logical to begin our investigation in an area of meaning which is itself in some sense inherently temporal. More than any

other category, the verbal lexicon appears to match this description best, for virtually any verbal process can be formulated in
such terms.

Having selected an initial area of investigation, the next question that arises is which items within the verbal lexicon we
should focus attention upon first. One of the most common
shortcomings of lexical semantic analyses, in my opinion, is that
the investigator initiates the analysis in a highly specialized sub-
section of the vocabulary, prompted no doubt by the conviction
that the more circumscribed the semantic field, the less likely one
is to become embroiled in vague abstractions that ultimately
vitiate the analysis. The outcome of such an approach, however,
is frequently less that rewarding because the terms of definition
remain too concrete and superficial, amounting at best to statements of only partial invariance which leave the truly invariant
semantic properties undiscovered. I have made this point before
(see above, pages 77ff), and reiterate it here because, with the
tools of analysis evolved so far through the study of grammatical
meaning, I believe we are now in a position to overcome this
major difficulty. Since we have developed a set of definitions
for some very basic semantic relationships, we should now be
able to look at the most basic or primitive terms in the vocabulary of verbal lexical meaning and begin our analysis there.

The brief descriptions provided below are intended only to
be suggestive of the ability of the present theory to handle such
conceptual properties as are displayed by the Russian verbal
lexicon. Research in this area currently in progress has already
identified more than 50 Russian verbs in terms of six features,
five of which appear to be identical to the ones we have already
encountered, except that certain adjustments have to be made
in order to accommodate the peculiarities observed in lexical as
opposed to grammatical meaning. Specifically, whereas grammatical categories are describable in terms of two sets, the narrated event and the speech event, a third set appears to be necessary when describing lexical categories. If all grammatical
concepts (and some lexical ones) are definable in terms of how
an observer who is situated in the speech event perceives the

events taking place in the narrated situation, most lexical concepts seem rather to be predicated upon how any observer, not necessarily one privy to the speech situation, perceives the given phenomenon. In other words, where grammatical categories are defined in terms of traditional — or better, "transmissional" — deixis which necessarily involves the speech situation (that is, the transmission of the message), lexical categories may be defined either in terms of transmissional deixis or in terms of another kind of deixis which, to use van Schooneveld's nomenclature, we may call "perceptional" deixis. In this latter form of deixis there is a relationship not only to an observer of the speech act but to any objectivized observer.[68]

The difference between the two types of deixis may be illustrated by comparing the verbs *stupat'* 'step' and *idti* 'go (determinate)' in Russian. In each of these verbs the subject moves from its initial position to a subsequent point which acts as the ultimate goal of the process. In both verbs the final point or destination is necessarily different from the original position of the subject, and therefore remains as the focus of the process — that is, the subject establishes a new position which remains in effect for an observer of the ensuing situation. Both verbs, in other words, are marked for extension, the feature that conjoins a phenomenon in the narrated event with its effect in the ensuing situation. What differentiates *stupat'* from *idti* is precisely how in each case the ensuing situation is defined. *Stupat'* merely means to take one or more steps in any direction, so long as the subject is elsewhere than its original position at the end of each step. Determination of the destination of the subject in this case is possible for any observer, whether privy to the speech situation or not. The meaning of the determinate verb *idti*, on the other hand, is tied to the speech situation in much the same sense that demonstratives are: the determinate verb points in a specific direction. The meaning of a determinate verb is inherently goal-directed and, significantly, when the actual goal of such a verb is expressed syntactically, it will occur in a case also marked for goal or 'directionality' (that is, extension): either the accusative or the dative. Thus we may conclude that *idti* is marked for ex-

tension with transmissional deixis, while *stupat'* is marked for
extension with perceptional deixis. What distinguishes these two
verbs from the corresponding indeterminate *xodit'* is that in the
latter, the final destination of the subject may or may not be
separate from its point of origin: in *xodit'* the subject may go
and return any number of times to its original starting point.
Xodit' is therefore unmarked for extension of either kind. All
three verbs, however, since they are verbs of motion, do have a
feature in common: verbs of motion are distinct from other
verbs in that their subject has always, at least initially, left its
starting point behind in performance of the process. As a class,
therefore, verbs of motion are marked for restrictedness of the
perceptionally deictic kind, since cancellation of the starting
point is not necessarily dependent on knowledge of the speech
situation for its identification. A determinate verb of motion (vs.
indeterminate) is then marked for both this form of restrictedness and transmissionally deictic extension, which latter feature
identifies the ultimate destination of the subject specifically
with reference to the speech act. We may diagram the relationships among the three verbs considered here as follows, noting
perceptionally deictic features with single primes and transmissionally deictic ones with double primes.[69]

	RESTRICTEDNESS'	EXTENSION'	EXTENSION"
xodit'	+	-	-
stupat'	+	+	-
idti	+	-	+

If, as this material suggests, there are two types of deixis, then
the number of feature oppositions in this system is twice what
we have been operating with so far. Furthermore, as we begin to
analyze lexical meaning, it will become immediately clear that a
sixth feature needs to be added to the five presented at the beginning of this section. This feature is 'transitivity', which does
not occur in any form of grammatical meaning. Transitivity is the
mark of lexically transitive verbs: the performance of a process
denoted by a verb marked for this feature leaves traces of its

existence on another object. We will have more to say about the nature and the place of this feature in the hierarchy of semantic concepts later. For now, suffice it to say that with the addition of this feature the system now contains twelve oppositions, and the number of verbs that may be distinguished by such a system is 2^{12}, or 4096 verbs.

We have already noted that with conceptual features such as the ones described here, we should be able to analyze the verbal lexicon beginning with the most basic (that is, unmarked) terms of the vocabulary. Determining which these are is not terribly difficult, for it seems intuitively obvious that the most basic concepts expressed by verbs in any language have to do with existence. It is not by accident, for example, that the classification of concepts in an English thesaurus commences with the various forms of being, and in Russian the verb 'to be' (*byt'*) certainly appears to be the term that expresses the most primitive type of verbal relationship, that of existence in its broadest, least specialized form. Moreover, the conceptual simplicity of the verb *byt'* in Russian is paralleled by its formal simplicity: as in many other languages it is left unexpressed in the present tense, thus coordinating a zero signans with a zero signatum. When the verb 'to be' **is** given formal expression in the present tense in Russian, the form that occurs is *est'*, but it is clear both from the formal disparity between *byt'* and *est'*, as well as from the more specialized nature of the occurrences of *est'*, that we have to do here with a separate and obviously more marked verb. *Est'* occurs specifically when the existence of something or someone is being asserted in the particular narrated event — that is, when the fact of the existence itself is the focus of the narrated situation. In other words, *est'* specifically establishes the existence of something for an observer of the ensuing situation: it is marked for extension.[70] Which type of extension is involved — i.e., whether the posterior observer is necessarily privy to the speech situation or not — appears to be merely a contextual variable in the case of *est'*, since both types occur: *est'*, for example, is the form used in answering a roll call in Russian, and in this context means 'here', which is clearly deictic to the speech situation; but in the context *Bog est'* 'God exists', the existence of God is reasserted for any observer. We may conclude, therefore, that the verb *est'* is marked for extension of the perceptionally deictic kind, which may or may not involve the speech act directly. (It should be obvious that, of the two types of deixis, the perceptional type is unmarked vs. the transmissional type, since the former may include the latter, but not vice versa.)

Looking back now at the relationship already discussed between *stupat'* 'to step' and *xodit'* 'to go', it is clear that we may establish the following parallel: *stupat'* is to *xodit'* as *est'* is to *byt'*. In each pair the first member is marked for extension, the second is not, much the same as in the case system where dative is to instrumental as accusative is to nominative. Parallels such as this are readily found throughout the verbal lexicon. If the feature of restrictedness denotes a phenomenon that does not last beyond its application in the particular narrated event, then the verb *minovat'* in Russian — which means 'to pass', not in the motion sense, but in the sense of 'discontinue being' — is marked for restrictednes vs. *byt'*. Similarly, *(u)meret'* 'to die' is marked for restrictedness vs. *žit'* 'to live', so that we have another parallel — *(u)mere't* : *žit'* :: *minovat'* : *byt'*.[71] The same relationship, it would appear, distinguishes *puskat'* 'to let' from *deržat'* 'to hold'; and so forth.[72]

Such parallel relationships as these (and there are many more that we could consider) strongly suggest that the verbal lexicon is as highly structured as any other linguistic category, and evidently operates with basically the same types of conceptual features as the various categories of grammatical meaning. This is the major conclusion I wanted to draw here. A great deal more evidence could be adduced in support of this conclusion, but I think sufficient groundwork has now been laid to suggest the degree to which this approach represents a fruitful methodology for the further investigation of lexical meaning. For a detailed accounting of the lexical structure of the Russian verb, the reader is referred to C.H. van Schooneveld, *Semantic Transmutations*, Vol. 2 (in preparation). Research currently in progress is concerned also with the structure of the nominal and adjectival lexicon of Russian, but rather than presenting any of this still somewhat speculative material at this point, I think it would be more valuable to consider a subject closer to the immediate concerns of current American linguistics: syntax. In the next chapter we will consider certain aspects of the structure of syntax and its method of analysis. We will return a second time to the subject of syntax in the concluding section of the final chapter, where I will present a more general outline of syntactic structure and its place in a theory of language as a system of signs.

CHAPTER FOUR

Syntax

1. THE SEMANTICS OF SYNTAX

Though it is certainly true that morphology and syntax represent
two relatively autonomous domains of linguistic structure, there
is once again no necessary reason to assume that both domains
do not participate equally in the sign function of language. So
frequently syntax is treated as a purely formal discipline in
contradistinction to morphology, yet it can be shown that in
each case we have to do with sets of formal properties associated
more or less directly with recurring elements of meaning. In fact,
what I shall try to demonstrate in this chapter is that the study
of syntax may be understood as the syntactic application of
essentially the same paradigmatic procedures that were outlined
above in the analysis of phonology and morphology.

To initiate this discussion, let us consider one of the major
categories of syntagmatic phenomena, that of word order.
Though it is obviously beyond the scope of this presentation to
attempt anything like an exhaustive treatment of such a broad
category as word order, certain general procedures for handling
word order phenomena as sign vehicles can be outlined. As at
any other level of linguistic structure, we proceed synthetically
(i.e., from the smallest element of syntactic structure to the
largest) and from the form to the meaning. On the formal side
we may observe that structure on the syntagmatic axis always at
least minimally involves sets of modification relationships whereby one part of speech modifies another. Thus adjectives modify
substantives, adverbs modify verbs or adjectives, and so forth,

culminating in the ultimate modification relationship, that of predication where, at least in the most common sentence type, a verb (or verbal phrase) modifies a substantive which functions as the subject or ultimate modified of the sentence, the thing about which something is said. Using this picture as a starting point, we may say that word order has as its basis a hierarchy of relationships between parts of speech acting as either modifiers or modifieds at different levels of concatenation.

Given this formal observation, we must next ask ourselves what semantic functions are fulfilled by the various formal relationships, for if syntactic phenomena are sign vehicles, they should display semantic properties just like any other set of linguistic forms. To determine how such modification relationships operate semantically, we may take one particular type and examine it more closely. I propose for the purpose of this discussion that we study the nature of adjectival and adverbial modification in three Indo-European languages: English, French, and Russian.

2. ADJECTIVAL AND ADVERBIAL MODIFICATION IN ENGLISH, FRENCH, AND RUSSIAN

In all three of these languages the modifying adjective may either precede or follow the modified substantive, but the semantic effect of the position of the adjective vis-à-vis the noun clearly differs in each case. If we study the difference between pre-position and post-position of the adjective in each language, it appears quite clear that we have to do with a binary opposition; one, moreover, which opposes a marked to an unmarked modification type. Pre-position of the adjective is obviously the more neutral, hence unmarked, word order in both English and Russian, whereas in French, post-position of the adjective represents the unmarked type. Let us look first at the situation in English. English grammarians all agree that the normal and most common position of the adjective is preceding the noun it modifies, and it is intuitively obvious that in this position the modification relationship remains neutral. Post-position of the adjective in English is considerably rarer in occurrence, and instances of this syntactic type are clearly more specialized in meaning. The question is: can we identify a common denominator of meaning for this latter type, that is, can we determine the nature of the semantic marking of adjectival post-position in English?

We can certainly arrive at a first approximation of such a marking, leaving a more refined definition for a later and larger study of the semantics of English syntax. For the moment let me suggest that when the adjective is post-posed to a substantive in English, it signals that the modification relationship is being specifically established in the situation described at the moment of speaking. That is, the nature of adjectival modification in such cases is deictic to the speech situation (whereas in pre-position such deixis may or may not be present). Several sub-types of the marked, post-posed type can be distinguished. The most obvious is predication, which is by definition a deictic category. In such a sentence as 'The boy is very smart', the smartness of the boy is specifically being established by the speaker at the moment of speaking, whereas in 'the smart boy' the modification relationship is presented as having been already established or at least presupposed. A second, closely related type is that of objective complement, as in 'The court declared the law unconstitutional' or 'They found the prisoner missing'. In the first of these two examples, the modification relationship is actually created by the action of the verb, and the reverse word order is consequently not possible: *'The court declared the unconstitutional law'. In the second example, both word orders are possible, depending precisely upon whether the adjective is understood predicatively or not: 'They found the prisoner missing' versus 'They found the missing prisoner'. A third type involves adjectival phrases where the modifier is additionally qualified in the situation described: cf. 'a complexion white as snow', 'a face wrinkled with age', 'men working in the field'. It is significant that when an additional, subjective qualification of the meaning of the adjective is made by the speaker, the whole modifying phrase is required to be post-posed in English.[1] Similar to the predicative types, this type involves modification which is deictically restricted or qualified. This deictic marking it would therefore appear, is the semantic invariant associated with post-position of adjectival modifiers in English, and predication, object complementation, and phrasal qualification are contextual variants of the general meaning of this particular syntactic property.

It should be noted that whenever an adjective occurs in post-position in English it carries this deictic marking, whether or not for a given contextual type a corresponding pre-posed variety exists. In other words – as we have observed in morphology – the formal category retains its constant meaning whether or not there is an opposition possible in a given case. Normally, the absence of a syntactic opposition points to a semantic incompatibility on the syntagmatic axis; that is, the very lack of opposition is itself a reflection of the impossibility of combining certain semantic properties, and is therefore proof that the semantic markings are in force. We need only look at a previous example to see that this is so. We observed above that the opposition of pre- and post-position occurs in the case 'They found the prisoner missing' versus 'They found the missing prisoner', but not in 'The court declared the law unconstitutional', nor in any other instance where only those adjectives are possible which, acting as objective complements, describe an object as it will appear specifically as a result of the action denoted by the verb. Such will be the case, for example, whenever the verb denotes some kind of causing or making, which requires that the complement be deictic or predicative: cf. 'The gift made her happy', 'The mud turned the water brown', 'She wrung the clothes dry'. Similar types can be found with verbs that denote attitudes and the like, as in 'He considered the man honest', 'I thought the story absurd', etc. In such cases the lexical meaning of the verb forces the choice, but whenever it doesn't, the possibility for opposition automatically returns: 'They stained the chair brown' versus 'They stained the brown chair'.

It is of critical importance to reflect for a moment upon the manner in which the preceding analysis is made. It is especially

significant that the analysis does **not** proceed from the traditional categories of attribution, predication, and so forth to observations about how the language expresses such categories. Rather,
our analysis proceeds in the opposite direction: from the observation of what formal devices are present in the language to
statements of the semantic content present in the formal material. Though it may seem that I am belaboring the point by
mentioning this methodological consideration again, the impact
that such procedural questions have on our understanding of
the nature of syntactic phenomena, it seems to me, more than
justify the repetition. Traditional analyses of both English and
Russian syntax, we might note, state that in each language attribution normally involves pre-position of the modifier and
predication requires post-position. But such a statement does
not tell us why, for example, in Russian virtually any attributive
adjective can also potentially be post-posed, whereas in English
such reversals are highly restricted. (I will return with specific
examples of this difference below.) One very obvious conclusion
to draw from such differences is that attribution and predication
are contextual reflections of the more general phenomena of
word order, specifically, the relative position of the modifier
and the modified in each language.

It might be countered at this point that the differences between English and Russian in such cases are merely a matter of
stylistics, but I do not think this is by itself an adequate response.
In the absence of a satisfactory definition of style, stylistics
becomes a catch-all category for linguisitc phenomena the semantic impact of which we do not understand very well. More
often than not conclusions about what is stylistic in syntax are
based upon statistical considerations, and these in turn are largely
a matter of choice of texts. Even though word order in Russian
is said to be stylistically free, whereas in English there are considerable restrictions, I do not believe the difference should be
accounted for merely in terms of the difference in function of
syntactic structures in the two languages. True, grammatical relations are primarily handled at the morphological level in
Russian, leaving the syntax relatively free to express more subtle

semantic differences, while in English the primary function of syntax appears to be to convey grammatical relationships. But the point is that whatever is expressed at the syntactic level in a given language, be it grammatical information or other semantic content, is governed by a single set of rules. These rules are themselves formulated as statements of invariant semantic markings associated with observable formal properties, and should explain not only why in English and Russian such contextual types as atttibutive modifiers usually precede their modified, while predicative modifiers follow, but also why in English attributive adjectives rarely follow the noun, whereas in Russian post-position of attributive adjectives readily occurs. Thus the rules, which are formulated as statements of invariance, serve also to explain the occurence of specific contextual variations. I propose that we now look more closely at the phenomena just described and illustrate the procedures outlined here in more detail.

In English, as we have noted, the post-position of attributive adjectives is highly restricted. We have already considered one such type, where the adjective is deictically qualified by the addition of a phrasal complement, and we may add a second type here, that of conjoined adjectives which add an element of subjective emphasis on the part of the speaker. In the latter case we find such examples as 'a man brave and strong', 'a look dark and menacing', 'lords spiritual and temporal', and the popular book titles, "All things bright and beautiful" and "All creatures great and small". It is noteworthy that this usage not only involves two conjoined adjectives, but the adjectives themselves have an evident semantic relationship between them, either one of antinomy or of reinforcement, frequently further enlivened by the incorporation of alliterative devices. All these facts point to the addition of a subjective coloring by the speaker which, while surely constituting a stylistic element, clearly falls within our definition of deictic marking for post-posed modifiers.

It is particularly remarkable in English that unless a deictic element is present, post-position of attributive adjectives does not occur. Even such cases as 'eyes closed', 'men working', 'shirt ripped', 'fly open', etc., are only possible when the adjective denotes a non-permanent quality of the noun, i.e., one valid specifically in the given utterance situation. Individual non-deictic attributes cannot be post-posed: *'pants blue', *'man decent', etc. As Bolinger has shown, we can use adjectives of a more permanent sort in this position only when the combination with the noun produces, in his words, something hypothetical, new, or surprising: 'people unconscious are unable to hear', 'Such countries friendly could be a great asset to us', 'Mary beautiful is something hard to imagine', 'A man unhappy is a social risk'.[2] Yet even here, the qualification has to fit the circumstances being invoked in the particular speech situation. One can say 'A man unhappy is seldom in control of his emotions', but not *'A man unhappy fell down and broke his leg'. The deictic marking is also most evident in the contrastive pair: 'present members' versus 'members present'. The lexical meaning of the word 'present' itself carries a temporal reference to the speech situation, so both examples are deictic to this extent, but the second phrase is doubly deictic, referring to just those members who are also members of the speech situation. Bolinger uses these examples to suggest that the meaning of the adjective in pre-position "characterizes" or "standardizes" the noun, while in post-position it shows "detachability from the noun."[3] Though this is certainly true, I do not believe such a formulation quite captures the essence of English adjective placement. For one thing, the notion of detachability from the noun also characterizes post-position of adjectival modifiers in Russian, as we shall observe in just a moment, yet there remains a significant difference in the usage of adjectives in post-position in these two languages. I believe that the marking for post-position in both languages is more restrictive than this, while pre-position produces a modification relationship which is simply unmarked, since pre-posed adjectives frequently have as one of their potential readings the reference that is produced by post-position.

In Russian, virtually any attributive adjective may be post-posed: *on čelovek porjadočnyj* 'He is a decent man' (adjective post-posed) is just as acceptable as *on porjadočnyj čelovek.*

Grammarians agree that post-position in such cases represents in Russian an inversion of the normal word order, i.e., is marked vis-à-vis pre-position. To determine what the marking is, we would have to look for a factor that would explain the relative freedom in Russian for post-posing virtually any adjective, whether the reference is specifically deictic or not. Obviously deictic reference still plays a role in post-position, for this is the word order normally used for predication in Russian: *krasivaja žensčina* (adjective + noun) 'the beautiful woman' versus *žensčina – krasivaja* (noun + adjective) 'the woman is beautiful'. Furthermore, inverted attributive modification frequently takes on what is sometimes called a predicative flavor in Russian: though the effect of the adjectival placement is difficult to render in English, a sentence like *na menja ona imela vlijanie sil'noe* 'She had a **strong** influence on me' shows, as the Soviet stylistician Rozental' suggests, that "the semantic load of the modifier is intensified, since its attributive meaning is complicated by a predicative nuance."[4] The Russian linguist Šaxmatov even calls this latter type of modification attributive-predicative, and notes that in such a case the adjective is presented as an accessory concept visualized separately from the substantive it modifies, suggesting the possibility that the substantive could have been modified by some other, opposite quality.[5]

These observations point to two things which fairly accurately describe the effect of post-posing attributive adjectives in Russian, and at the same time explain the normal use of this word order for predication. They are a greater degree of **independence** of the adjective from the noun it modifies, which results in **intensification** of the meaning of the adjective. In van Schooneveld's words, "the reference to each of the two members [noun and adjective] is much more independent; the paradigmatic opposition (in lexical meaning) to the other members of the same word class [adjective] is, as it were, intensified."[6] Since predication implies independence of reference — the relationship between the modifier and its modified being established by virtue of the speech situation itself — it is natural that predication would normally occur in post-position. When an attributive adjective is post-posed in Russian, its lexical meaning is intensified because it is presented as not being so closely tied to the concept expressed by the noun it modifies. The feeling of "predicativity" in such cases is a natural consequence of the marking of greater independence: due to the looser association with its modified, the adjective appears to take on special significance in the given narrated situation. But predicativeness is a highly impressionistic term for the semantic property we are describing and is best avoided, in my opinion, because of the false associations it may suggest with other types of semantic relationships. In particular, predication is technically a deictic concept, yet as soon as we compare the Russian evidence with the situation in English, we can appreciate that deixis does not adequately characterize the range of usage associated with the marked word order in Russian. Predication is one of the major contextual variants of postposition in Russian, just as it is in English, but it is not the Gesamtbedeutung in either language.

When adjective placement is understood as a binary opposition, and the real invariant of the marked member is identified, the occurrence of the modifier in either position can be explained, whether we are dealing with a stylistic inversion or a word order perceived as being "normal" for a given type of modification. This is particularly important for Russian where almost any word order could be labeled stylistic, except for the very basic rule that attributive types tend to be pre-posed and predicative types post-posed. Post-position of the modifier in Russian is the more restricted, marked type in which the paradigmatic, lexical meaning of the adjective is intensified by its relative independence from the noun it modifies. Hence predication normally utilizes the marked word order, as does attribution whenever the meaning of the adjective is foregrounded. Pre-position of the modifier in Russian is unmarked, and the lexical meaning of the adjective in this position may or may not be intensified. Usually, of course, it is not, as in the stylistically neutral cases of attribution; but it also may be, as when a predicate modifier is pre-posed. Even in the latter case, however, pre-position of a predicate modifier usually engenders a weakening of the paradigmatic

opposition of the lexical meaning normally associated with an
adjective used predicatively, sometimes, as van Schooneveld suggests, resulting in anaphora of the modifier: cf. *soldat – xrabryj*
'the soldier is brave' (stylistically neutral, semantically marked
grouping) versus *xrabryj – soldat* 'brave is the soldier' (semantically unmarked grouping, anaphora of the modifier).[7]

Though these observations are of a necessarily preliminary
nature -- for one thing, the markings for both Russian and
English need more exact definition based upon a larger corpus
of material — they nevertheless point the way to a radically different view of syntactic analysis, one that does not require the
postulation of a separate set of abstract formal structures to explain the relationships among syntactic elements. Operating with
a model which treats all syntactic structures equally as sign vehicles allows the statement of syntactic relationships without
adding a separate level of deep structures which, from the point
of view of sign theory, constitutes a "phenomenologically unwarranted multiplication of entities."[8] As a phenomonology of
language, sign theory treats all so-called surface forms as partici-
pating equally in the informational content of utterances. Far
from being impoverished, as Chomsky likes to say, these surface
data actually carry meaning just as any morphological form does,
and it is the task of the linguist to determine what the network
of informational elements is that is reflected by the surface
forms. If the term deep structure is warranted at all, it should
be constituted by the hierarchy of semantic relationships that is
represented by the various levels of modification in the constituent structure of a sentence. I will elaborate further on the role
of constituent structure in Chapter 5, when I present the outlines of a general theory of syntax. In preparation for this larger
discussion we need to consider some of the implications inherent
in what has been said so far about syntactic phenomena. One
conclusion we ought to draw is that if the relationship between
attribution and predication is indeed based upon a semantically
marked versus unmarked binary opposition, then current attempts to treat attribution as a syntactic process derivative from
predication are semantically counterintuitive, since such a pro-

cedure amounts to deriving the unmarked syntactic configuration from the marked one in languages like English and Russian. The preceding analysis suggests that, rather than being derivative the one from the other, attribution and predication are both part of a more general (abstract) process of modification which, as van Schooneveld proposes, lies at the heart of all syntactic phenomena. His approach, which I am adopting in principle here, leads to the conclusion that syntactic structures are governed primarily by a hierarchy of modification relationships among the various parts of speech in a given language.[9] I have intentionally limited the foregoing discussion to adjectival modification of substantives in order to simplify the presentation, but once the data base is broadened, it becomes clear that the nature of modification is defined not only by the order of elements, but also by the relative markings of the constituents of speech themselves. Let us look for a moment at the four major parts of speech and begin to sketch a broader picture of syntactic relationships.

Verbs and substantives are marked in opposition to adverbs and adjectives respectively, in that the former present "an element of exogeneous reality **in its entirety**," that is, not just as a quality of an action or a thing, but as the action or thing itself. In this respect adverbs and adjectives, being unmarked, may or may not have this property: thus adjectives, for example, normally denote qualities, but may also function as substantives. In addition, substantives and adjectives are marked in opposition to verbs and adverbs respectively, in that the former denote "an element of exogeneous reality whose existence is ascertainable **independently of the time of transmission** [i.e.,] **of the speech situation**." In this respect adjectives are marked because even when used predicatively, they continue to denote qualities ascertainable independently from the moment of speaking, while verbs are unmarked because, though they usually carry a deictic category (tense, person, etc.), they do not have to (cf. infinitives). With these two sets of marking relationships, therefore, we obtain the following picture:

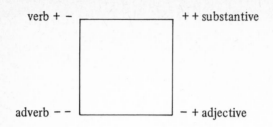

verb + –   + + substantive

adverb – –   – + adjective

With these relationships in mind, we may note that, in syntactic combination, the relatively unmarked parts of speech normally modify equally or relatively more marked ones: adverbs modify adjectives and verbs and in a few cases nouns, adjectives modify nouns, and verbs modify nouns (verbal predication); in addition adverbs may modify other adverbs, a noun another noun (genitival modification), and so forth. This observation may be restated as a general grammatical rule, that a modifier (whether attributive or predicative) usually belongs to an equally or less marked (lower) word class than its modified. In the case of Russian we may further specify a semantic (syntactic) rule, that **post-position of the relatively unmarked or lower word class constitutes the semantically marked word order**, for the phenomena associated with adjectival modification discussed above actually represent part of a much more general phenomenon which holds true for all the major parts of speech in Russian. In adverbial modification, for example, we may compare *bystro govorit'* (lit: 'quickly talk') versus *govorit' bystro* ('talk fast'): the latter word order is clearly marked in Russian again by the relative independence and intensification of the meaning of the adverb. Likewise, *vezde izvestnyj* (lit: 'everywhere known') versus *izvestnyj vezde* ('known everywhere'). Furthermore, as in the case of adjectival predication, verbal predication in Russian normally utilizes the semantically marked word order, where post-position of the unmarked word class (the verb) is necessitated by the independence of reference inherent in predicative modification. Stylistic inversions of subject and verb tend, as we noted above in the case of adjectival predication, to weaken the independence of the lexical meaning of the modifying verb: e.g. *prišel Ivan* 'Ivan came' where the verb is taken for granted and all the emphasis is focussed on the subject.

It also appears that a similarly general rule applies for modification relationships of the various parts of speech in English, where **post-position of any lower-order word class is marked for deixis**. With adverbial modification, for example, we may note that in contradistinction to Russian, where adverbs can be freely pre-posed or post-posed in accordance with the marking of independence and intensification, English again puts greater limitations on adverb placement, just as it does with the adjective. Adverbs in English tend to precede verbs when they qualify the action as any action would be qualified, but they follow the verb when they qualify the particular action as it is performed in the particular situation. Thus in a sentence like 'He spoke foolishly about the incident' the adverb tells us something about what he said, that is, about the manner in which the verb was performed, while the corresponding sentence 'He foolishly spoke about the incident' implies that it was a mistake for him to talk, though what he actually said might have been quite sensible. In general, post-position of manner adverbs in English is required because this type of adverb produces by definition a deictic modification situation; and conversely, adverbs which cannot be given a deictic interpretation cannot be post-posed in English. Thus in the sentence 'He finished the job poorly', 'poorly' can only be interpreted as a manner adverb and consequently has to follow the verb, while in the sentence 'He never finished the job', 'never' cannot be interpreted as a manner adverb and must precede the verb. Adverbs of time and place also as a rule establish deictic situations and are therefore normally post-posed: 'They live here', 'He went home early', and so forth. A sentence like (?*) 'I would help you gladly' sounds a bit strange because the adverb does not qualify the action of the verb as much as it characterizes the disposition of the subject; hence 'I would gladly help you' is much preferred. For the same reason, imperative constructions in English nearly always require the adverb to be post-posed, for in such types the modifier specifies how the action is to be performed in the given situation: 'Speak more slowly', 'Read this carefully', 'Calm down'. In many cases splitting infinitives is such a common "mistake" in English because **not** to split the infinitive frequently forces the adverb behind the verb whether the situation is deictic or not. Here the formalistic grammarian's rule runs counter to the native speaker's intuition which is governed by the semantic markings. Cf. 'A man she resrespected too highly to tease deliberately' versus 'A man she respected too highly to deliberately tease'.[10] The first example suggests that she might still tease him but not intentionally, while in the second example she is not likely to tease him at all.

Bolinger has noted that adverbs commonly precede the verb in English when they denote the obvious way of performing the action, as for example, in 'He was badly shaken (cut, bruised, wronged, surprised)', 'He politely held the door for me', 'He rudely insulted me', etc. By contrast, the same adverbs when post-posed denote something unusual about the way the action is performed: cf. 'wrote the paper badly', 'constructed the house poorly', where 'badly' and 'poorly' are not the normal ways of performing the given processes. Bolinger suggests a "standard" versus "non-standard" dichotomy in such cases, but I think rather that this distinction is once again a direct reflection of the deictic marking of post-posed modifiers. Non-standard simply means that the attribute is not the usual sort of quality that would be applied to the verb in question, but is one that the speaker imposes upon the verb in the given utterance situation. Furthermore, standard adverbs can also be post-posed whenever the speaker wants to draw attention to the manner in which the process is performed in the given situation: 'He was bruised badly' emphasizes the seriousness of the situation; 'He held the door for me politely' suggests that he didn't do it merely out of a sense of duty; and so forth.

I believe we have some very strong evidence here for a general principle of syntactic structure: that the order of constituents in a sentence is in large part a reflection of the semantic marking associated with the relative position of modifier and modified at each level in the hierarchy of constituents in a given language. I say in large part because we have been operating here in abstraction from certain phenomena which obviously play a role in the semantics of modification, most particularly prosodic elements. Still, I think we are completely justified in studying such a subtle mechanism as modification in terms of how it is affected by the operation of one formal property at a time. To test these conclusions further, I would like at this point to consider evidence from yet another language, French.

Modification in French is particularly interesting because the marking relationships are the reverse of what they are in English and Russian. Post-position of the modifier constitutes the neutral or unmarked word order in French, while in pre-position the meaning of the modifier is clearly marked. When pre-posed the French adjective, for example, assumes a noticeably subjective quality in the sense that its meaning appears to be intimately tied to that of the noun it modifies: "l'adjectif épithète se place *avant* le nom lorsque, sans être entrée dans la syntaxe figée, la combinaison **adjectif + nom** est très fortement sentie comme une unité de pensée. [. . .] L'adjectif se place *avant* le nom quand il a une valeur qualitative, exprimant un jugement, une impression, une réaction subjective, souvent affective."[11] Consider the effect of the relative position of one and the same adjective in the following contrastive pair: *poète heureux* versus *heureux poète*, both of which mean 'happy poet', but in slightly different senses of the term.[12] In the first instance we have to do with a poet who is happy as any person might be happy, but in the second, where the adjective is pre-posed, the happiness refers to the individual specifically insofar as s/he is a poet, and we would most likely translate the second example as 'successful poet'. Likewise in the pair *homme pauvre* versus *pauvre homme*, the former refers to a man who is poor in some more or less objective sense, e.g. for lack of money, whereas in the latter, pre-posed type the poorness has to do with just those qualities that make a man a man, so to speak (i.e., in the sense of 'poor bloke'). Again, in the pair *avantage réel* versus *réel avantage* the adjective 'real' qualifies the noun in the most general sense when post-posed, while in pre-position the kind of reality referred to is just that necessary to satisfy the conditions of something being an advantage, e.g. that it is large enough to be significant. The distinction in this last pair can perhaps best be appreciated by considering what would constitute the reverse of the two situations: the opposite of an *avantage réel* would be a *faux avantage* 'false advantage', whereas an advantage that is not a *réel avantage* is a *petit avantage* 'small or inconsequential advantage'. And finally, consider *ami vieux* versus *vieil ami*; in post-position the adjective refers to the age of the person, whereas in pre-position it refers specifically to the duration of the friendship. Hence *un vieil ami* could very well be a relatively young person.

Based upon the evidence in these examples, we can rephrase our previous statement and suggest the following, more precise formulation for the semantic marking associated with pre-position of adjectives in French: when the adjective precedes the noun, it **presupposes the lexical meaning of the noun it modifies**. This formulation not only captures the essence of what distinguishes pre- from post-position in contrastive pairs such as those described above, it also provides an explanation for why certain adjectives in French occur almost exclusively in one position or the other, allowing contrast only in the rarest instances. Consider those adjectives which occur predominantly in pre-position: they are all modifiers whose lexical meaning subsumes an especially wide range of contextually determined variants, such as *grand* 'big, great, tall, large', *petit* 'small, little, dear, cute', *beau* 'good, beautiful, admirable, noble', *mauvais* 'bad, wrong, false', *joli* 'pretty, charming, considerable', and so forth. To determine what the specific referent of such an adjective is in a given context, one has to first identify the noun that is to be modified. To determine 'largeness', for example, one has to know what sort of object is involved, for a large table is considerably smaller than a large house. Adjectives that denote colors are among those which occur predominantly in post-position in French, since the qualities they give are quite objectively definable. But occasionally such adjectives do precede the noun, in which case they assume what appears to be a metaphorical connotation: cf. *noire*

ingratitude, noirs pressentiments, verte jeunesse, blanche neige,
etc. With the definition proposed above for the marking of pre-
posed adjectives, we can specify in technical linguistic terms just
what it means to say that such a usage is metaphorical: even
those adjectives whose meanings are relatively concrete or objective may be pre-posed when the quality they express is likened
to the specific attributes given by the lexical meaning of the
noun they modify.[13] This same observation also explains the
pre-position of adjectives when they serve as so-called epithètes
de nature, as in *la pâle morte, le bouillant Ajax*, and so forth.
Here, as above, the adjective gives overt expression to a quality
which describes the essence of the particular noun.

There are a number of adjectives in French whose meanings
in pre- and post-position are sufficiently far apart that most in-
vestigators prefer to label them different adjectives. In this category we may include the adjective *mauvais* already mentioned
above, which in pre-position frequently means 'wrong' and in
post-position 'bad'; *simple*, meaning 'simple' in post-position,
but in pre-position 'mere'; *ancien*, which has the connotation
'ancient' in post-position, while in pre-position frequently means
'former', and so forth. Formally speaking, of course, we have to
do with the same adjective in each position, so the question is
whether our definition of the marking associated with pre-position can account for the apparent disparateness of meaning in
a manner sufficient to justify classifying the two usages as
contextual variants of a single adjective in each case. Consider
first the adjective *ancien*. This adjective carries the connotation
of something not just old, but old in the sense that the object
modified is perceived as being qualitatively different from the
way the same object might appear in the present. In other words,
implied in the meaning of *ancien* is a break in continuity as re-
gards the status of the object it modifies, and when *ancien* is
used in post-position this quality is presented as applicable more
or less equally to any object. In pre-position, on the other hand,
the same quality is presented in terms relative specifically to the
nature of the noun being modified. Hence *l'ancien régime* 'the
old-style regime' refers to an older form of government that has

since been replaced by another form of government; *ancien français* 'Old French' refers to an older form of the French language that has been superseded; and *ancien ami* 'former friend' implies a break in the friendship over time. Notice that in each of these cases where the adjective precedes the noun, one has to know something about the nature of the noun itself in order to infer the sense in which it is old. There is nothing objectively definable as 'old' about Old French – only in relation to the features of modern French can Old French be described as old. And much like *vieil ami* discussed above, *ancien ami* refers specifically to a quality of the friendship as opposed to the person involved. But the uses of this adjective in both positions are obviously related by the common lexical meaning of oldness producing a qualitative change in the status of the modified, so we are certainly justified in calling the differences in usage contextual variants of one and the same adjective. By the same token, the adjective *simple* in post-position denotes a quality of being uncomplicated that can be measured more or less objectively, while in pre-position the same quality is presented as ascertainable only when measured specifically against the nature of the object modified. Hence the connotation 'mere' in pre-position, which implies the simplest form of whatever qualities are inherent in the object itself. In this position *simple* may also mean 'alone' or 'just', as in *croire quelqu'un sur sa simple parole* 'take someone on his word alone'. Here again it is specifically the meaning of the noun modified that establishes what is simple about the process.

Moving now to predicative modification, we may note that the normal position for predicate adjectives in French, as in English and Russian, is following the noun. Obviously, therefore, there is no necessary correlation between the usage of the marked word order and predication, since French utilizes the unmarked order for this type in contradistinction to both English and Russian. What the evidence from these three languages does suggest, however, is that the normal position for predicate modifiers will correspond to that word order which provides semantically the greater degree of independence of the modifier from the modified. In both Russian and English it is the marked word order which provides the necessary independence – in the form of intensification in Russian and deixis in English – and consequently predication normally occurs as a contextual variant of this type. In French, on the other hand, the marked word order all but precludes independence of reference, the referent of the adjective in this position being semantically tied to the noun it modifies for its very recognition. Hence in French predication appears normally as a contextual variant of the unmarked word order, where the adjective is post-posed. This is not to say, of course, that predicate modifiers can never precede the noun in French; they occasionally do and when they do, much the same as in English and Russian, the subject modified is usually presented anaphorically: cf. *grande fut sa surprise* 'great was his surprise'; *fière est cette forêt* 'proud is this forest'; etc. The anaphoric quality in these examples is a direct consequence of the marking associated with pre-posed modification in French, where the lexical meaning of the modified is presented as already established or presupposed in the situation described.

If we look now at adverbial modification of verbs in French, we cannot but be struck by the fact that the same observations that were made with respect to adjectival modification appear once again to hold true. It is significant that in French the adverb generally follows the verb it modifies (the unmarked word order) with one notable exception: in constructions with the so-called composed tenses, which consist of an auxiliary verb and a past participle. In these cases the normal position of the adverb is immediately preceding the participle, which is just what one would expect given the fact that the participle is the one verb form that presents the action as an established fact: cf. *J'ai toujours pensé qu'il avait raison* 'I always thought he was right'. Here the adverb modifies the participle as an element whose lexical meaning is presupposed in the situation described. The one major exception to the placement of adverbs before participles is with adverbs of location: *Il est allé là-bas* 'He has gone there'. One possible explanation for this fact is that adverbs of location do not qualify the manner in which the action of the verb takes place. Unlike other types of adverbs, they thus do not modify the verbal process in a manner that would allow them to be pre-posed, since they do not present a quality that could be inherent in the lexical meaning of the verb. Rather, it is in the very nature of adverbs of location that they present additional information which is relatively independent of the verbal process. Also one should bear in mind that the position of post-posed modifier represents the unmarked word order in French, and shifts to this word order from the marked word order are considerably more frequent than are shifts in the opposite direction. It is no doubt quite significant that French adverbs may occur before participles (which are, semantically speaking, adjectives), but rarely if ever do they occur before any other verb form. (The only other regularly pre-posed types are the two pronominal ad-verbs *y* and *en*, which present special semantic problems of their own.) It would appear, therefore, that there exists some sort of semantic incompatibility between the marking associated with the marked word order for modification in French and the markings associated with the verb as a part of speech (see above, page 123). The nature of the incompatibility in this case, I would suggest, involves the fact that the verb — being marked only for presenting "an element of exogenous reality in its entirety," and not being marked for presenting "an element of exogenous real-ity whose existence is ascertainable independently of the time of transmission [i.e.,] of the speech situation" — does not, there-fore, present a phenomenon whose existence can be assumed in the situation described. Only when it is presented as a participle (i.e., an adjective) does the action of the verb assume the quali-ties necessary for such presupposition, and only then do adver-bial modifiers regularly precede. The kind of syntactic restriction evident here provides an excellent example of how semantic compatibilities and incompatibilities determine the nature of syntactic structures.

Other instances of adverb placement require a rather more involved explanation as, for example, when the adverb in any one of the languages we have discussed is placed in immediate initial position in the sentence, presumably for purposes of miseen-relief. In these and other instances where the adverb occurs at some distance from the verb it modifies, we probably have to do with the above invariant qualities complicated by additional factors, among them rhythm and euphony, and other devices motivated in part by the structure of the text itself. Just how such devices are incorporated into or reflected by the semantic structure of syntax must remain for the time being a subject for further study.

With this analysis of word order phenomena we have, of course, by no means exhausted the study of syntactic relations, but we have embarked upon the explanation of one of its most critical components and have, I hope, firmly established the thesis that even such a set of surface formal properties display a consistent correlation with semantic invariants defined in a language-specific context. As far as language-specific semantic invariance in syntax is concerned, we may yet take up the question of government, which is a topic of particular value in the present context because of the frequency with which it is treated as a purely formal phenomenon devoid of any semantic relevance.

3. A SEMANTIC APPRECIATION OF GOVERNMENT AND AGREEMENT

Russian is a language in which verbal government of the case of the objective complement plays an especially prominent role, and therefore provides ample opportunity to study the semantic nature of this type of syntactic relationship. We have already considered the semantic markings of the various Russian case forms, the determination of which is a necessary prerequisite to the study of this type of government. In the discussion of the Russian case system above I made the point that we must not view the phenomenon of verbal government as occasioning a semantically empty use of case forms, even though there may be in some instances no choice of case allowed by the verb in whose context the nominal complement appears. It is absolutely essential in linguistic analysis that we distinguish carefully be-

tween phonological and morphological elements when considering the question of redundancy. Phonological oppositions may
indeed be neutralized in certain environments, since their semantic function does not extend beyond the signalization of
"mere otherness". When mere distinctiveness is neutralized, no
other semantic content remains, and we are justified in writing
purely formal rules to express this type of contextual conditioning. The function of morphological elements, on the other hand,
is not limited to the expression of distinctiveness. The formal
constituents of language at the morphological level are endowed
with their own meaning, so that when used redundantly such
elements lose only their distinctive capacity in a particular context, not their meaning. For this reason, writing purely formal
rules to express redundancies in syntax is not justified. Rather,
the very motivation behind the restrictions in usage in such cases
should be sought in the semantic content of the constituent
forms.

It is at this point that the notion of semantic compatibility
plays an essential role as the motivating force behind the occurrence of syntactic configurations. If only one case type normally
occurs as the complement of a certain set of verbs, it is because
the given case is the one semantically compatible with the particular lexical type of verb involved. For example, verbs in Russian
which require objects in the genitive case comprise a semantically
identifiable set distinguishable from verbs which allow only
accusative objects, and so forth. Verbs that take genitive objects
in Russian form a relatively homogeneous semantic group in
which the action expressed does not allow complete attainment
of the object by the subject. The verbs included in this set have
such meanings as 'strive for', 'avoid', 'be afraid of', 'desire', and
so forth. This set may include as well virtually any verb under
negation. That the objects of such verbs should normally be in
the genitive case follows directly from the fact that the genitive
is marked semantically for the feature of 'quantification' (or
'objectiveness' in van Schooneveld's terms), which specifies that
the case referent (the phenomenon denoted by the noun) does
not participate fully in the action of the verb, but maintains its

'objective' existence outside the situation described. However, should the reference to the noun be of a highly specific nature, as when the reference is to a specific object already established in the context of the utterance, the case of the noun frequently switches to the accusative – the case which stipulates that the noun is the focus of the verbal process: cf. *ja ne čital ètu knigu* [acc.] 'I haven't read that particular book'. Since in the latter context both the genitive and the accusative are potentially possible (*ja ne čital ètoj knigi* [gen.] also occurs) I can conceive of no purely formal, syntagmatic device capable of capturing the difference between the two utterances. The difference – slight though it may be in such cases – clearly derives from the intent of the speaker and is made on semantic grounds – in this case involving the degree to which the object is made the focal point of the process, which is a conceptual distinction encoded in the set of paradigmatic relationships that define the structure of the Russian case system.

The above example illustrates, moreover, that the kind of redundancy expressed by verbal government is by no means absolute, there frequently being a choice for a given verb of at least two types of complements usually involving different cases, with or without prepositions. This gives us all the more reason for insisting that the case forms retain their invariant meaning even under conditions of redundancy. The extent of the selection process with respect to verbal government in Russian is such that semantic criteria must be invoked to sort out all the contextual possibilities, for the degree of complexity evidenced by the number of syntactic combinations allowed is simply too great to be handled by purely formal devices. Only by investigating the paradigmatic structure that lies behind the selection process can we hope to explain the subtleties in usage that are the genius of the Russian language.

As with the phenomenon of verbal government, so, too, with prepositional usage in Russian the evidence suggests that the choice of the case in which the regimen occurs is semantically motivated, even though the number of cases governed by a given preposition is strictly limited. Thus, for example, the Russian preposition *o* 'about' (in the sense of 'concerning') occurs almost exclusively with the locative case, but may also appear with the accusative whenever it denotes contact with the object, as in *udarit'sja o kamen'* 'hit against a stone'. In the latter instance the object is necessarily directly involved in the process and the use of the accusative, marked only for 'directionality' (i.e., focus on the object), is clearly semantically motivated. Likewise the motivation for the fact that the preposition *čerez* 'through, across' governs only accusative objects is clear: for the process to pass through the medium of the object (whether concretely or abstractly), the object has to be directly involved in the process. The degree of involvement is obvious in such examples as *čerez les* 'through the forest' and *čerez ulicu* 'across the street', which involve motion through or to the other side of a concrete object; it is just as evident when the object is more abstract, as in *čerez čas* 'in (after) an hour', where the period of time denoted by the regimen is necessarily used up in the establishment of the process, hence also totally involved; and in such types as *peredat' pis'mo čerez sestru* 'send a letter through one's sister' (i.e., have the sister deliver it), where the process cannot be accomplished without the direct involvement of the sister. In the latter case one might argue that there is just as much involvement evident in the sentence *pereslat' pis'mo po počte* 'send a letter via the mail', where the construction *po* + dative replaces *čerez* + accusative, but the fact that 'sister' is human and 'mail' is not plays a certain role in this case with respect to the degree of involvement: the inanimate object is perceived more as merely an instrument, whereas the animate, human one is not. Cf. *xodit' po ulice* 'to walk along the street', where the street acts merely as the conduit for the process, and assumes no active involvement in it. The difference here can be underscored by observing that the expression *čerez počtu* also occurs, and would tend to be used when the speaker wished to emphasize the special role of the post office in the process of transmission, as, for example, if he had made a special effort to get to the post office to mail the letter, or if there were some problems specifically created by the mail service. Again it must be emphasized that the difference noted here between the prepositional phrases *čerez* + accusative and *po* + dative is not always directly reflected in the facts of the extra-linguistic situation to which these phrases may refer in a given context. The difference is a linguistic one, codified in the semantics of the prepositional and case systems of Russian, and frequently represents no more than a difference in the **mode of perception** of an event in external reality. We must remember that the distinctions being described here are inherent in the structure of the language, and are reflected in the structure of events only insofar as a given language selects certain aspects of a situation over others for expression. It is not, therefore, a legitimate challenge to the conclusions being drawn here to say that either phrase could be used in a particular context with "little or no difference in meaning". For the difference in meaning cannot be established simply by observing the characteristics of a single physical event or series of events. It can only be established by observing the range of events signalized by a particular linguistic form to determine what they have in common. That is to say, semantic analysis must proceed from the set of signantia in a given language.

If verbal and prepositional government produce considerable restrictions on the choice of case forms in a language such as Russian, the degree of syntagmatic restriction on the co-occurrence of grammatical categories evidenced by the phenomenon of agreement is still greater. Yet even here we can see that semantic considerations play an indispensable role. Even with such a relativley straightforward phenomenon as verbal agreement as to person, taking Russian again as an example, the redundancy displayed by verbal grammatical endings vis-à-vis subject pronouns is once more far from absolute. To appreciate the nature of the selection process at work in this case, one has to pay attention to whether the subject pronoun is present or absent. In Russian, *oni govorjat* means 'they say' with a reference to an identifiable antecedent for the subject pronoun, whereas the same construction minus the pronoun, *govorjat*, may mean either 'they say' in the sense of the first example, or in the sense of 'one says' with no specific or identifiable referent for the implied subject, a connotation which the former construction cannot have. The ranges of reference are clearly different in these two examples, and therefore we have to conclude that the presence or absence of the pronoun has definite semantic import. What this evidence suggests is that the person marker on the verb (the verbal grammatical morpheme) makes a general stipulation as to person (first, second, or third), while the personal pronoun adds a second reference to an indentifiable subject. Each form — grammatical desinence and pronoun — thus carries its own independent meaning despite the echo effect of the person designation on the verb whenever the pronoun is present.

This observation is of especial importance for the grammar of Russian, where subjectless impersonal constructions constitute one of the major sentence types of the language. In these constructions the implied subject is a generalized third person singular 'it', the identity of which is left formally unexpressed: cf. *mne ne spitsja* 'I can't sleep' (lit., 'to me (dative) [it] doesn't sleep (reflexive),); *mne dumaetsja* 'I would think' (lit, 'to me (dative) [it] thinks (reflexive)'); *možno kurit'*? 'Is [it] allowed to smoke?'; *mne xolodno* 'I am cold' (lit., 'to me (dative) [it] is cold'); etc. Though a large portion of these impersonal constructions include a dative complement, we would be missing a significant semantic generalization if we concluded merely that the subject of the sentence is expressed syntactically by the dative case. What each of these constructions has in common is the indication that some outside force (the unexpressed grammatical subject 'it') is the proper agent of the action expressed by the verb, and the logical subject ('I' in the above examples, in the dative case) is in essence the indirect recipient of the action — the indirect goal of the process. In all of these impersonal types the action takes place despite the efforts of the logical subject, and the set of grammatical relations — in particular the overt expression of case — provides this semantic information directly, while the lack of specification of the action's real source is "expressed" by the absence of a subject pronoun (zero signans). The fact that the invariant semantic characteristics which unite such constructions into a single sentence type in Russian in accordance with their formal means of expression are frequently lost in English translation and can only be recovered through a variety of circumlocutions (such as the use of different modal auxiliaries and the like) should have no bearing on how we analyze the Russian material. Careful observation of the functional value of each of the formal means of expression in a given language provides the key to linguistic analysis just as much at the syntactic level as anywhere else.

The conclusions being drawn here are further borne out by consideration of when the subject 'it' (*èto*) may receive formal expression in Russian and when it may not. In contrast to English, 'it' in Russian is expressed by *èto* only when there is an identifiable antecedent present in the situation described (cf. *oni* 'they' above). Whereas in English one says 'It is a pity that. . .', 'It is raining', etc., Russian does not allow the pronoun in these cases: *žal'*, *čto*. . . '. . .is a pity that. . .'; *idet dožd'* 'rain falls'. Only when the pronoun corresponds to the demonstrative 'this, that' does Russian allow formal expression of such a subject: *èto moja kniga* 'It (this, that) is my book'; *č'ja èto kniga* 'Whose book is it (this, that)'. Once again, therefore, the presence versus absence of a formally expressed subject pronoun in the syntax of Russian carries specific semantic information.

This concludes the present discussion of syntactic phenomena. I will return to a consideration of general principles of syntactic structure at the end of the next chapter, after introducing some additional concepts central to the understanding of syntax.

CHAPTER FIVE

Meaning in Perspective

1. ABSTRACTNESS, INVARIANCE, AND THE DEFINITION OF SEMANTIC FEATURES

Now that we have had the opportunity to observe how semantic properties operate to explain the occurrence of not only grammatical and lexical categories but also a variety of syntactic structures, we can return to a consideration of some of the general questions raised by this type of analysis. Perhaps the most obvious of these concerns the degree of abstractness inherent in the type of conceptual features proposed here, and the corresponding problems that arise as to their verifiability. Such concerns are, of course, by no means new, but have been voiced with respect to this kind of analysis rather persistently over the years. It is surely true, for example, that Jakobson's original analysis of the semantic structure of the Russian case system has received less attention by semanticians than it might otherwise have at least in part because of these problems. One need only recall that in the rebirth of concern about semantics that occurred in American linguistics in the mid 1960s, Jakobson's approach received almost no attention at all. Even a linguist as familiar with the theories of the Prague School as the late Uriel Weinreich dismissed this entire approach as misguided in 1966 in a rather curt sentence or two, claiming that the "mechanical" postulation of a class meaning for such a heterogeneous grammatical category as a case results in "empty[ing] the notion of class meaning of all content."[1]

It is also significant, however, that much of the reasoning

Weinreich invoked at the time in making his statement would no longer be supported by many linguists today. His remarks about Jakobson, whom he singled out as "the most eloquent exponent" of the class meaning point of view, were presented as an illustration of the bias inherent in claims that, for example, **everything** in syntax is semantically relevant. In contrast to this "extreme" position Weinreich pointed to the occurrence of "completely meaningless patterning" in language, and especially to transformations and morphophonemics, two areas which many linguists would now agree do indeed carry a great deal of semantic information. An ever increasing number of American linguists are currently engaged in serious studies aimed at determining how to incorporate relevant semantic information at virtually all levels of grammar. And in this sense the approach I am outlining here is nothing more than an attempt to advance this general trend to its ultimate and obvious conclusion: the realization that surface forms carry semantic information directly, the principal function of language being to convey information of one kind or another.

While allowing that the referential (cognitive or designative) function is not the sole function of language, the present study seeks to determine just how much and what kinds of cognitive information are present in surface linguistic forms in the sort of normal language use where the referential function is predominant. The point of departure in such a study, therefore, has to be the assumption that there is no "completely meaningless patterning" in language. Obviously such a hypothesis represents a statement about what would be considered the **ideal** state of language from the point of view of linguistic sign theory.[2] And the extent to which individual language systems depart from this ideal state is a matter for empirical investigation. Formal entities which are indeed meaningless in a given language will be shown to be so by the impossibility of finding recurring semantic properties that correlate with them. No a priori statements to the effect that transformations, morphophonemic alternations, or any other elements of natural language are meaningless need be made (and risk having to be retracted at a later date).

In this context there is only one thing that separates the "extreme"position being put forth here and other positions regarding the semantic content of linguistic forms. No one denies the value of investigating the purely formal patterning of language, but this exercise should not be construed as an end in itself. Rather, the study of invariance on the formal side simply needs to be complemented at every stage by an equally intensive investigation of the semantic correlates of this formal patterning. In other words, investigation into the formal properties of language is a necessary prerequisite to semantic analysis.

It is in just these considerations that we find our initial response to the problem of abstractness in the study of meaning. In the present approach the patterning of formal elements is precisely what provides the basis for the investigation of semantic regularities in a given language. The methodological priority of what I have called formal determinism insures that the very nature of semantic categories — their type and number, as well as the degree of abstractness associated with them — will be determined by the primary (formal) data of the language itself. Therefore, once again no a priori decision need be made concerning what semantic categories are present in a given language, nor how abstract these categories ought to be. The entire process of semantic investigation is thus put on the most empirical footing possible for a study of conceptual elements. And if it turns out that the range of semantic variation associated with certain types of formal elements (for example case categories as they are evidenced in actual grammatical morphemes in a particular language) is broader than we are accustomed to dealing with under the rubric of a single invariant, that in itself is not sufficient reason to abandon the formal criterion. Rather, we should be looking for the appropriate tools for handling such highly abstract conceptual categories, preferably criteria that have already been proven valid in other domains of linguistic science (e.g. phonology) and in other branches of science.

The one indispensable tool which answers to the precise needs of this type of analysis is the topological principle, successfully applied in the extraction of invariance at the phonologial level by Jakobson. As we have described above in preceding chapters, topology is the relational construct by which even highly disparate variables can be united into a single invariant through the determination of a recurrent, common property or set of properties. What makes this concept such an ideal candidate for handling the highly abstract categories inherent in semantic analysis is precisely its capacity for relating the individual instances of a more general phenomenon, which individual occurrences may themselves be heterogeneous in character. One of the most revealing illustrations of this principle is the perceptual experiment involving chickens reported on above (p. 57). The chicken is trained to peck on the lighter of two color fields, one gray and one dark. When the two individual fields are replaced by a pair, one gray and one light, the chicken switches its pecking to the light field. The chicken realizes full well that what is gray in one context may very well be light in another, since what it has learned is the abstract, relative invariant of light vs. dark. Yet for some reason we as linguists still balk at allowing for just such relativistic judgments in semantic analysis. This reticence is all the more difficult to understand when we realize that semantic selection also involves the identification of perceptual categories, just as does the chicken experiment, not to mention the discrimination of distinctive sound qualities. As I shall demonstrate in more detail below, semantic categories are themselves perceptual categories, and experiments on human perception do convincingly demonstrate "the categorial nature of perceptual identification," whereby "we come to identify constancies, treating as equivalent objects that have been altered drastically in all respects save thier defining attributes."[3]

Thus if the genitive case in Russian, for example, signalizes such disparate types of usage as the partitive, the direct object of a negated verb under conditions of non-specificity of the object (i.e., lack of focus on the object), the object of an affirmative verb signalizing striving for or avoiding, as well as other contextually conditioned variants, there should be no hesitation in assigning them all to a single semantic invariant, provided of course that the invariant represents a systematically recurring meaningful element in the language, the essence of which can be determined to reside in each of the contextually conditioned usages.

The concept of topology thus legitimizes the search for true semantic invariants and effectively eliminates the problem of abstractness per se in a formally based study of meaning. With this basic problem out of the way, we can concentrate our attention on the more serious issues that are engendered by a methodology which attempts to operate with such highly abstract elements. I have in mind here two related problems, first the difficulty of defining in a rigorous and non-impressionistic manner the common elements of meaning extracted by such an analysis, which brings us to the ultimate issue, that of the verifiability of such features. These two points are really two sides of the same coin, and therefore need to be discussed in the same context. In order to do this, I propose that we look at how the definitions of some of the features discussed in the preceding chapters have evolved historically from the time of Jakobson's first introduction of them in the thirties, through the refinements they have undergone in the work of van Schooneveld during the past couple of decades. This evolution shows a clear trend towards increasingly technical definition and concomitantly towards greater verifiability, but what is more important, we can observe in these refinements the application of certain principles which put semantic analysis on an increasingly rigorous scientific footing and point the way towards what promises to become a true calculus of meaning.

When Jakobson originally proposed a set of three features to define the invariant semantic relations extant in the Russian case system, he described each case type primarily in terms of how the noun in question relates to the process denoted by the verb **in the situation described in the sentence**. Thus the feature 'directionality' was assigned to a noun which functioned as the goal or focus of the process denoted by the verb in the given narrated event; 'marginality' defined any noun whose function was the accompanying circumstance of the verbal process in the situation being described, and 'quantification' posed the question of the degree to which the phenomenon denoted by the noun participated in the events being described, if at all. There was an obvious suggestion here that case relationships semantically represented varying degrees of involvement of the noun with the verbal process, from a maximum of total involvement in 'directionality' to a minimum in 'quantification', where the involvement could be reduced contextually to zero. The possibility of a hierarchy of features was thus implicit in these definitions, though none was suggested (at least in print) by Jakobson at the time. It was not until further investigation had been made of the possible recurrence of these features in other grammatical and lexical categories of the Russian language that a more precise statement of the relationship among the features and their place in a larger, more complex hierarchy of conceptual elements could be made. This process necessitated a substantial redefinition of Jakobson's original three features, a redefinition which resulted in nothing less than the establishment of an entirely new framework upon which to base the concept of conceptual categories in language. It is this framework that I wish now to elaborate upon because it is one of the major contributions of van Schooneveld to linguistic science.

What van Schooneveld saw as the key to a more general definition of conceptual features such that the presence of one and the same feature could be identified in a variety of different grammatical or lexical categories, was the need to shift the description of the common property defined by a feature out of the immediate context of the situation described – that is, extract it from its immediate syntagmatic conditioning – and put it on a more general (i.e., paradigmatic) footing. Otherwise it is impossible to determine, as we have seen, what there is in common between two concepts such as the 'marginality' inherent in the instrumental case, which denotes the instrument or accompanying circumstance of the verbal process, and the 'restrictedness' that marks such prepositions and preverbs in Russian as *pere-*, *ot*, *vy-*, and *iz*, which imply the cancellation of a previously existing situation (see above, pages 96 ff). Even within the case system itself, for that matter, certain constructions defy explanation if the basis for the analysis is restricted to the set of relations that exist within the narrated event alone. Jakobson foresaw this difficulty, obviously, in his treatment of examples of the type *èk ego zalivaetsja* 'look how he burst into voice', where it is the **subject** of the sentence that is in the accusative, the case marked for goal or focus of the process. Here the accusative cannot be the goal of the process denoted by the verb in the given narrated event, but must be the focus of some other process, namely the speech event represented by the intention of the speaker.[4] Here for the first time we have a case relationship being defined semantically on elements not in the narrated situation, but in the speech situation. This same shift in perspective provides an explanation for such case usages as the so-called ethical dative, which directly involves the addressee of the speech situation in the events of the narrated situation: e.g. *tut vam* (dative) *takoj kavardak načalsja* 'here began (for you) such a confusion'; cf. English "Now there's an old car for you." As Jakobson suggested, the ethical dative explicitly defines the content of the utterance to its receiver: the hearer is perceived as if he were affected by the verbal process, as if it had even taken place with reference specifically to him.[5] In other words, the addressee of the speech situation fulfills the function of the indirect goal of the process denoted by the verb in the narrated event, the dative case being marked for both directionality and marginality.

Van Schooneveld's contribution to the development of this line of reasoning was the realization that not just certain case relationships, but all of the semantics of case — and, ultimately, all grammatical (as opposed to lexical) meaning in language — should be defined with respect to the speech situation. That is, grammatical meaning in general is deictic to the speech situation, since ultimately it is the speaker who decides from what perspective the events he is describing will be presented, and he manipulates the grammatical categories of his language accordingly. In other words, grammar (as opposed to lexicon) evaluates the significance of a particular segment of extra-linguistic reality for the participants of the speech situation. We will consider

how other grammatical categories than case are deictic in just a
moment. For the present, let us look at how, specifically, the
individual meanings of each of the case features may be redefined
with this new perspective on the nature of grammatical meaning.
The concept of 'focus' in the feature of directionality (e.g. in
the accusative case) involves, from the point of view of the
speaker, a branding of the object in such a way that the effects
of the focus in the narrated situation **extend** into the speech
situation, that is, remain as a focal point for the speaker and
addressee. Thus not only do utterances such as *èk ego zalivaetsja*
establish a link to the speech situation, but any accusative usage
in Russian does. Cf., for example, the careful selection of case
forms in such constructions as *podarit' emu* (dat.) *rubl'* (acc.)
'to give him (dat.) a ruble (acc.) as a gift' versus *podarit' ego*
(acc.) *ulybkoj* (inst.) 'to favor him (acc.) with a smile (inst.)',
where the use of different case forms forces a specific interpretation on the addressee as to how he is supposed to view the relative effect of the objects involved: direct and lasting in the accusative as opposed to indirect and transient in the instrumental.
In the feature of marginality, which marks the instrumental case,
the effects of the relationship established in the narrated event
between the object and the verbal process do not extend beyond
the narrated situation itself, but are **restricted** in their validity
to the situation described. Hence the transient nature of the
instrumental in the above example and the purely adverbial
quality of so many other instrumental usages in Russian. The
dative, the case of the indirect object, which in Russian is marked
for both of these features, can also now be defined in more
precise terms: a dative object functions as the focus of the process denoted by the verb in the narrated situation only so long as
the process itself lasts. Thus what may at first sight appear to be
a cumulation of two contradictory features in fact produces a
clearly definable semantic relation.

Before redefining the third of Jakobson's case features in these
terms, we need to look for a moment at the nature of the hierarchy that is established between the first two. Rechristened
'extension' and 'restrictedness' respectively to reflect the essence

of the deictic connections they each entail, these two features now clearly seem to be ordered with respect to one another. The extension feature first establishes the connection between the speech event and the narrated event, while restrictedness then cancels this relationship, that is, restricts the applicability of the phenomenon to the narrated event alone. On the premise that a relation has to be established before it can be cancelled, we ascertain that the order of the features is as presented. What is especially significant here is that the very type of semantic concepts we are operating with virtually predicts the necessary ordering. Because our semantic concepts are defined in terms of elements that describe logical categories out of which language itself is fundamentally composed – the speech event and the narrated event – the types and the ordering of the features, it appears, follow a natural, logico-linguistic progression.

This observation is rather strikingly borne out by consideration of the third of Jakobson's case features, which he called 'quantification'. In his terms, quantification poses the question of the degree to which the phenomenon denoted by the noun is involved in the verbal process, if at all. Such a phenomenon, if it does not exist in the narrated situation, or if only part of it does, must therefore derive its existence from somewhere else. Since neither the narrated event, nor obviously the speech event, can be the source of such a phenomenon, there is logically only one place left from which this type of concept can originate, and that is the stock of semantic elements in the language itself. In other words, in an utterance such as *dom otca* 'father's house', the father – which in Russian is in the genitive case, marked for quantification – may be maximally remote from the events described in the narrated situation. For example, the father's role in these events may involve nothing more than the fact that he owns the house. His existence, therefore, may in no way derive from participation in the situation described, but only from the fact of the word 'father' having been invoked. Likewise, when one says *boga net* 'God (gen.) does not exist', the existence of the concept of God can only be derived in the final analysis from its existence in the lexical semantic stock of the language.

Summarizing these observations and putting them into strictly deictic terms, we may say that the speaker has one of three choices for categorizing how he may interpret the role that a nominal element plays in Russian: either its effect will be perceived as extending into the moment of speaking (extension), or the speaker may present the phenomenon as restricted in its effect to the time of the situation being described (restrictedness), or he may perceive the phenomenon as objectively ascertainable independently of either the moment of speech or the situation described (in our revised nomenclature, objectiveness). Thus the feature of objectiveness completes the hierarchy begun with extension in the case system of Russian, invoking a third conceptual element which has its source in the inner workings of language itself.

The nature of the features induced from this reexamination of the grammatical system of case in Russian now seems to be established in such a way that the systematic recurrence of any one of them in other grammatical categories can be adequately tested. So, for example, when we look at the tense system of the Russian verb, we can determine whether the same features are operative there or not. In Russian the category of tense is quite restricted, there being at best only three types: past, present, and future. I say at best because the future in Russian is not represented as a separate morphological tense: it is expressed either as a derivative of the distinction in aspect (perfective present = future in this type) or by a compound – that is, syntactic – form (conjugated from of the verb 'to be' + imperfective infinitive). Therefore, as far as tense as a morphological category in Russian is concerned, we really have to do with a single binary opposition between past and non-past forms. Let us look at this opposition first, and return later to the analysis of future time and aspect.

In the tense opposition the non-past is clearly the unmarked member, just as the nominative is in the case system of Russian. Like the nominative, the non-past tense maintains a relation to to the speech situation without specifying what the exact nature of the link is. A true tempus aeternum, the non-past may refer to an event which occurs simultaneously with the moment of speaking or it may not. Much the same as the unmarked simple present tense in English, this form has connotations which may refer to the present, past, or future. The preterite, on the other hand, is limited to the expression of either of two types of verbal relationship, one where it denotes actual anteriority to the moment of speaking, and the second where it signalizes a hypothetical event. The fact that a number of languages use the same tense form to indicate both of these two types of meaning strongly suggests a common semantic property between them, one, moreover, that is very naturally captured by the feature of restrictedness we have been considering. If we step back for a moment from such traditional semantic notions as 'anterior' and 'hypothetical' and view these two types of usage from the perspective of the strictly linguistic categories we have defined, we can see that what the two types of preterite have in common is that the narrated event cannot be perceived simultaneously with the perception of the speech event. Either the narrated event occurred at some time prior to the moment of speaking, or its occurrence takes place only in a hypothetical situation which, precisely because it is hypothetical, also cannot be taking place at the moment of speaking. Thus the preterite is marked specifically for the fact that the link with the speech situation (established in general for the category of tense by the nonpast) is cancelled. The preterite, then, is to the tense system what the instrumental is to the case system: the phenomenon denoted by the form is valid only in the situation described; it is marked for **restrictedness**.[6]

The concept of future, on the other hand, though it, too, appears to stipulate lack of simultaneity with the moment of speaking, does so in quite a different way. A future tense presents the occurrence of some event more in the sense that the genitive case presents a phenomenon: its existence is stipulated purely on the basis that its perceptibility, and hence the possibility of its occurrence, exists objectively; i.e., by virtue of its existence in the set of verbal concepts in the language itself. Whereas the preterite gets its meaning by presupposing, as it were, the existence of the narrated event (whether past or hypothetical) and then stipulating that this event cannot be perceived simultaneously with the moment of speaking, either because it occurred at some moment prior to speaking or because it occurs only in the mind of the speaker, future time represents a reversal of this logic: in the future the narrated event has no prior existence either in time or in the mind of the speaker, but its occurrence is still asserted. Thus in a language with a separate morphological future, some form of the feature **objectiveness** would probably be operative, though how the exact marking of such a form would manifest itself in a particular language will, of course, depend upon what other forms are also present in the verbal morphology of the language in question. In Russian, however, the concept of future time is intricately tied up with the concept of aspect, so that we cannot analyze the forms involved without also considering what role aspect plays in the determination of future time.

The aspectual distinction — perfective versus imperfective — operates in both the past and non-past tenses in Russian. In both instances the perfective is marked versus the imperfective: it signalizes that the verbal process has specific limits, expressed contextually as a beginning and/or an ending which separates the process from both the speech situation and any other verbal process that may occur in the context of the narrated event. The marking of the perfective aspect is thus **dimensionality**.[7] When used with the past tense the perfective always implies at least that the process has been completed, and the emphasis in the utterance is therefore not on the performance of the process itself, but on the result(s) that it produces. The limits expressed by the perfective in conjunction with the past tense may also, however, refer to the beginning of the process, as, for example, in reporting a sequence of actions where the start of a subsequent action depends upon the completion of a prior one for its realization. In such a situation both processes are expressed by perfective verbs in Russian, unless there is in the context a specific indication of the manner involved or of the time spent in performing the process, in which case the imperfective would reappear. When used in conjunction with the preterite, the dimensionality of the perfective aspect is reinforced by the restrictedness of the marked tense form, so that we get a kind of double separation from the moment of speaking: one that produces the connotation of anteriority (tense) and the other which signalizes completion and production of a result (aspect).

When used with non-past tense forms, the limits or dimensions of the process invoked by the concept of perfectivity nearly always point at least to the beginning of the process, thereby automatically implying future time in most instances. The combination of perfectivity and a non-past verb form cannot refer to an event occurring simultaneously with the moment of speaking, since the concept of present time necessarily indicates an ongoing process that has already been initiated. A process actually taking place at the moment of speaking can only be expressed in Russian by an imperfective verb. Even when a perfective non-past form does not refer to future time, it still cannot refer to a real act taking place simultaneously with the moment of speaking. In all the other contextual usages of this form there is a reference either to a sporadic action which is presented only as a potentiality, to a denial that an action does occur, to the presentation of an action in a sequence of historical events, or some other act (such as a habitual one) similarly divorced from perception simultaneously with the act of speech.[8] Clearly, then, the limits or dimensions that the perfective aspect puts on the process in non-past as well as past tense forms separate the verbal process from co-occurrence with the moment of speaking. In recognizing the essentially deictic nature of aspect as well as tense, therefore, we have made another significant modification of Jakobson's original views on the role of deixis in language, illustrating once again the inherently deictic character of all grammatical meaning.[9]

Continuing the discussion of future time in Russian, we have seen that one type of future is clearly derivative from the distinction in aspect: it is the major contextual variant produced by the combination of the marked aspect with the unmarked tense (perfective non-past forms signal future time in most of

their contextual usages). The second type of future in Russian
presents a somewhat different picture. It is a syntactic construction composed of a conjugated form of the verb 'to be' and an
imperfective infinitive. As the use of the imperfective aspect
suggests, this construction signifies emphasis on performance of
a process in the future. It is close in both form and meaning to
the English 'shall, will be doing', and thus differs from the
perfective non-past form described above, which has more the
connotation of 'shall, will initiate an action or accomplish something'. It seems to me there are two ways one could analyze the
compound imperfective construction, and I will simply present
them both here as equal possibilities. On the one hand one could
say that the conjugated form of the verb 'to be' in Russian is a
perfective, non-past form itself, which would automatically explain the future meaning of the construction and put the analysis of this type of future completely in line with the previous
type, explaining both futures as derivative from aspectual distinctions.[10] The verb 'to be' in Russian, *byt'*, lacks a normal set
of conjugated forms in the present tense, which is what one
would normally take to be imperfective. The only fully conjugated set of forms that exist, with the root *bud-*, produce the
future construction, so there is some justification for calling
them perfective. But not all analysts agree on this point. Van
Schooneveld, for one, prefers to view the root *bud-*, as an
imperfective form which is **lexically** marked for objectiveness,
so that the concept of futurity in this type would be explained
as the output of a lexical and not a grammatical marking.[11]

Whichever of these two analyses of the Russian compound
future ultimately turns out to be preferable is not crucial to the
present discussion. What remains important is the fact that we
have now succeeded in establishing the basic framework for an
objective and verifiable analysis of grammatical properties in
language. We have demonstrated that the recurrence of one and
the same conceptual feature in more than one grammatical category is objectively ascertainable, provided that the semantic
properties themselves are defined in rigorously linguistic terms —
that is, by utilizing the logic inherent in language itself, and

holding strictly to the formal criterion for the determination of the range of contextual variation subsumed by a given invariant. The indispensable key to the success of this analysis has been the broadening and deepening of our understanding of the concept of deixis, which now takes its place along with invariance and opposition as one of the cornerstones of the present approach. Still, however, we have only scratched the surface in our consideration of what the concept of deixis implies. For one thing, we have only looked so far at the role that deixis plays in the determination of grammatical meaning. We need to further our understanding of this key concept in order to fully appreciate the extent of its impact upon semantic analysis.

2. THE ROLE OF DEIXIS IN SEMANTICS: MEANING AND PERCEPTION

Deixis has traditionally been used to identify such types of linguistic elements as adverbs like 'here' and 'now' which require knowledge of the spatial and temporal setting of the moment of speaking for their identification; pronouns such as 'I' and 'you' which assume knowledge of who the participants in the speech situation are for their identification; categories of tense which in traditional analysis are viewed as involving the temporal relationship between the moment of speaking and the events being described; and so forth. In the foregoing section we refined the analysis of tense as a deictic category in this sense, and in addition we broadened the application of the concept of deixis to include other grammatical categories such as case, in a language which has a morphological case system, where it is apparent that the way in which nominal elements are presented is also codified with respect to how they are to be perceived by an observer of the speech situation; and aspect, where the question of simultaneous perception of the verbal process and the moment of speech assumes the role of defining characteristic of the category. If this analysis is correct, then it would appear that the codification of elements of *parole* into *langue* is far from an occasional process, but is one which is central to the whole edifice of semantic structure, at least as far as grammatical meaning is concerned. We should ask ourselves, therefore, just what it is that a speaker does when he codifies elements of his own act of speaking.

What makes a category deictic in the sense that this term is normally used is the fact that the speaker makes a reference to the act of speech he is about to engage in. That is, he perceives himself as a potential observer of his own anticipated act of speaking, and he has done so over a period of time so that he has codified certain elements of this process of perception. In other words, he has a preconceived idea of himself and others producing utterances. What is especially important in this formulation of the essence of deixis is that the speaker is presented as treating the speech event as something to be observed just like any other event about which he might think or speak. The speech event is thus one possible type of perceivable event in the mental (linguistic) life of the speaker. And a deictic category in the traditional sense may be defined as a category of meaning where an anticipatory reference is made (by the speaker) to elements of this particular kind of perception event.

As used by the Greeks, the term deictic meant 'demonstrative' or 'pointing', but it has been generalized and at the same time localized in linguistics to refer to a variety of categories that involve the indication of elements present specifically in the act of speech (cf. Peirce's indexical signs). The process of linguistic pointing, however, is really equivalent to the very act of making reference, which of course occurs each time we speak, but is not limited to the identification of elements of the speech act alone. The act of reference is itself a deictic act, whether we refer to the speech event or any other event in extra-linguistic reality. Thus we may say that **all** meaning in language is deictic in the sense that the creation of semantic categories is the result of a constantly self-renewing process of making reference through acts of perception to the world around us. What creates categories of meaning in language is the fact that the speaker has codified (generalized from) his own acts of perceiving reality. Reality to the native speaker is nothing more or less than the cumulative effect of a series of acts of perception, and the ability to speak is predicated upon the speaker's having generalized from these acts of perception to create a system which allows him to communicate about what he perceives. Every time he speaks (makes reference to extra-linguistic reality) the native speaker anticipates and therefore recreates his own act of perception. This is the real essence of deixis, which is therefore one of the most fundamental properties of the human capacity to speak.

Thus we may redefine deixis as **the anticipation of an act of perception**, of a perception event. The speech event is a particular kind of event which is perceivable just as is any other event, but it is one which in language is obviously elevated to a very special status. Therefore the speaker's anticipated reference to his own act of speaking creates a special kind of deixis, one for which we can reserve the term TRANSMISSIONAL DEIXIS. This term will correspond to the traditional concept of deixis in the extended form elaborated above. This is the kind of deixis which dominates the structuration of grammatical meaning. All other forms of reference – i.e., those in which the perception operation does not necessarily involve the speech event – may simply be referred to with the term PERCEPTIONAL DEIXIS. In this, the more general type of deixis, the speaker anticipates his perception of some aspect of external reality other than the speech event per se. This is the kind of deixis we see at work, for instance, in the various categories of lexical meaning.

As an example of how deixis operates in the determination of lexical meaning, we may return for a moment to consideration of the Russian verbal lexicon, a rudimentary sketch of which was begun in Chapter 3. In a language such as Russian (and apparently English works the same way) the lexical morpheme of the verb provides information about the status of the *agens* in intransitive verbs, or of the *patiens* in transitive verbs, at the end of the verbal process **as compared to its status before the process began**. That is, the lexical meaning of any verb signalizes how the *agens* or *patiens* is to be perceived once the action of the verb has been fulfilled, but the nature of the final status can only be conceived by comparing it with the initial status from which the process originated. It is this deictic, anticipatory reference to the perception event represented by the situation that pertains at the beginning of the verbal process which underlies the operation of verbal lexical features. Individual lexical morphemes are marked semantically in different ways depending upon how the situation at the end of the process relates to the initial situation.

In Russian, for example, the lexically unmarked verb is clearly *byt'* 'to be', where no specific information is given as to the status of the *agens* at the end versus the beginning of the process. The two states are, as it were, equivalent. However, if we consider the verb *minovat'* 'to pass (in time), be over, leave behind', we see the same semantic element present, mutatis mutandis, that we saw on the grammatical level in the preterite (versus the present tense). The verb *minovat'* may be either transitive or intransitive, and the dictionaries list it as being either imperfective or perfective (though there is a purely perfective form *minut'*). We can conclude, therefore, that this verb is unmarked for both transitivity and perfectivity, and its only marking seems to be lexical (perceptionally deictic) restrictedness, for it refers in all of its somewhat varied contextual usages to a situation of mere being (*byt'*) which ceases to exist at the end of the process: cf. *zima, burja, opasnost' minovala* 'winter, the storm, danger passed'; *čtoby minovat' bolota, my sdelali bol'šoj obxod* 'in order to avoid (pass by) the swamp, we made a large detour'. In both the transitive and intransitive types of *minovat'*, the verb signalizes a situation in which an original instance of *byt'* has been cancelled. Thus, just as the mark of transmissionally deictic restrictedness in the preterite presupposes (anticipates) the link to the speech situation established by the unmarked non-past tense, similarly the mark of perceptionally deictic restrictedness in the verb *minovat'* presupposes a relationship to the initial situation predicated by the unmarked member of this minimal lexical opposition, represented by *byt'*. This same type of relationship holds, mutatis mutandis, with respect to the *agens* in the verbal pair (*u*)*meret'* 'to die' which is lexically marked for

restrictedness versus *žit'* 'to live' (unmarked). In this pair
(u)meret' implies an initial situation of *žit'* that has been cancelled. By the same token, we obtain yet another set of minimally distinct pairs, where the resulting situation pertains this time
to the *patiens*, and which are all therefore additionally marked
for transitivity, in the following examples: *davat'* 'to give'
(marked for restrictedness) versus *imet'* 'to have' (unmarked);
puskat' 'to get (go)' (marked) versus *deržat'* 'to hold, keep', and
so forth. In Chapter 3 we observed that the class of motion verbs
as a whole in Russian is also marked for perceptionally deictic
restrictedness, the meaning of all of these verbs denoting an
initial starting point that is left behind by the process, hence
cancelled.

Thus, provided that we view the lexical meaning of the
Russian verb in terms of how the situation produced by performance of the process relates specifically to the situation that
existed before the process began, we can begin to establish the
fundamental features of such a lexical system in objectively
definable, strictly linguistic terms, the key in this case being the
realization that semantic relations are deictic even when no specific reference is made to the speech situation per se. At this point
one might argue, I suppose, that what are termed perceptionally
deictic categories here are not really deictic in the same sense
that traditionally deictic ones are because the latter involve a reference to a specific, semelfactive situation which the perceptional
types appear to lack. On the one hand we have a reference to an
element in a particular speech situation, while on the other (in
the case of the verbal lexicon) the reference is to a situation
whose existence is presupposed as the starting point of the verbal process. What makes these two types of reference equivalent,
however, is the fact that language operates, as I have been
suggesting, on the plane of **perception**: linguistic acts are themselves acts of perception, and this implies that reference in language is not made to things, but to the perception of things. It
is in this sense that the act of perceiving an element in a particular speech situation is no different from the act of perceiving
the situation that initiates a particular verbal process. In both

cases we have to do with a semelfactive act of perception, an individual act repeated every time we speak.

In fact, it is only by realizing that language is in the final analysis the cumulative effect of such individual deictic acts of perception that a structural semantics can possibly extricate itself from the dilemma of having created a *sui generis* system of language, one that is impersonal and self-regulating. This realization is what establishes the requisite link between an otherwise closed linguistic system and the various spheres of extra-linguistic reality upon which it impinges, especially the external world of events to which linguistic forms refer. Jakobson foresaw this solution, I believe, when he suggested that the traditional distinction between meaning and reference be replaced by the more fruitful dichotomy of general versus contextual meaning (see above, pages 49ff). Jakobson realized that the concept of reference as it is traditionally employed in linguistics and logic leads the semantic investigator into an impasse: either he ends up classifying elements of exogenous reality in their own – that is, in non-linguistic – terms, as the biologist classifies trees, or he locks himself squarely in the "prison-house of language" by the creation of a closed linguistic system. With his phenomonological approach Jakobson insists that a linguistic utterance has truth value not because it coincides with something in the external world (real or imaginary), but rather because its existence can be affirmed in terms of its "modes of givenness", which "exist" precisely because truth statements can be made about them: e.g. "The gods eat ambrosia, they don't drink it." For Jakobson, all reference is in the final analysis situational context; that is, language refers not to things but to the appearance of things in particular contexts. And this is precisely what is implied by a conceptualization of meaning in terms of acts of perception.

The conceptual features proposed in this study all categorize **modes of perceiving** external reality; they do not categorize external reality directly. What is critical here is that one's perceptions of reality do not have to coincide with any particular elements of reality, yet at the same time they are not divorced from reality either. Rather, perception is one plane of reality, and it is the realization that language operates on this plane that provides the necessary link between language and the external world. Thus as far as language is concerned, it is utterly irrelevant that the morning star and the evening star "refer" to the same element in the real universe. This fact by itself is of interest only to the scientist in us. What is relevant to language is the fact that the two different **appearances** of the planet Venus have enough cultural significance to be afforded separate modes of expression. Ultimately all reference in language is made to the appearances of objects and not specifically to any objective qualities those objects may possess. Thus whether two items are the same or different in the real world has no bearing on whether they will be perceived as the same or different in a particular language. In the real world any two items may be compared and considered either the same or different. We can add apples and oranges any time we like, as long as we decide to make the equation at a sufficiently abstract level, because the possibility to equate or not to equate in the real world is constrained only by the choice of category. When we seek to describe languages, therefore, we ought to be concerned with the choice of categories that has already been made by the language in question, the evidence for which exists in its surface forms. Thus, whereas in English we distinguish between 'butter' and 'oil', Russian has only one lexical item to signal both concepts: *maslo*. On the other hand, Russian distinguishes between *syr* 'non-curd cheese' and *tvorog* 'curd cheese', while English has only one general concept for both. This suggests that there is no non-arbitrary way for the linguist to categorize the conceptual universe to which languages relate without having recourse to the perceptual categories that underlie the selection process in each language.

Viewing a particular synchronic state of a language as the cumulative effect of a series of perceptional acts also allows us to account in the most natural way for the dynamic aspect of synchrony. If, as I have suggested, each act of speech requires a new act of perception, then the synchronic system of a language is automatically open at all times to reinforcement or intervention from the outside in every speech situation. I see no other way to view language than as a two-way street: on the one hand it is obvious that our perceptions have been pre-categorized by a history of previous linguistic associations — the invariants of our language determine to a large extent how we will perceive future events. But it is just as obvious that these very invariants have to be constantly reinforced in order to survive. To the extent that they are not reinforced they change, and the idea that language is governed fundamentally by deictic acts of perception accounts for both possibilities. The process of relating to the external world (through perception) is repeated each time we speak, thereby either reinforcing (regenerating) or revising our perceptual categories.

This same approach to meaning also provides a solution to the problem of how to reconcile the existence of idiosyncratic connotations given particular words by an individual speaker because of his personal experience or associations, and the generally accepted (dictionary) definitions held more or less in common by the speech community as a whole. Every individual lives both in his own private world and in that of his culture, and we are all at times misunderstood as we attempt to relate our personal experience to that of those around us through the process of communication. This fact, however, merely demonstrates that the individual's deictic acts of perception are in constant interplay with those of other speakers. What creates the sociological fact of language is the degree to which this interplay produces equivalent perceptions, and hence equivalent linguistic categories, which is the prerequisite of communication. Obviously the linguist cannot hope to describe the perceptual acts of every individual native speaker in a speech community, but he can productively investigate the common set of perceptions held by the community as a whole without running the risk of describing merely an abstract fiction. The common set of perceptions is just as real as any individual set, and the proof of this is found in every successful act of communication.

3. SIGN THEORY AND SEMANTIC UNIVERSALS

The foregoing observations have a bearing not only on how we conceive of the study of meaning, but also on the question of semantic universals (which for many linguists is the same thing). The issues here may be put into clearer focus by considering the following. Since there are apparently no languages that a linguist today would call primitive, linguists are in agreement that all languages are capable of expressing a substantial body of universally held experience. Only the means of expression seem to differ from language to language, and this has led a great many linguists and logicians alike to treat the study of semantic universals — and indeed semantic investigation in general — from the perspective of how certain types of concepts are mapped onto the formal means of expression in different languages. In case grammar, for example, it is assumed that there is a set of semantic concepts which can be subsumed under the rubric of "case relations" which exist in all languages, whether or not there is a consistent mode of expression for such a set of concepts in any particular language. These concepts are then mapped onto a variety of different formal means of expression — including not only overt case morphemes, but both overt and covert syntactic relationships as well — by a set of abstract rules. The issue that must be raised with respect to this kind of analysis concerns the selection of the concepts that are presumed to be universal. In the first place, the kinds of "case" relations proposed — e.g. agentive, instrumental, objective, factitive, locative, benefactive, and so forth[12] — bear little resemblance to the sorts of conceptual relationships that are consistently signaled by case forms in languages which possess overt case systems. At best they coincide with certain of the contextual applications of such forms, as can readily be ascertained from the analysis presented in various places in this study, which suggests that the concepts associated with case forms in a typical case language like Russian are a great deal more pervasive and subtle than those proposed in case grammar. If this is so, then where do the concepts in case grammar come from, and on what basis are they proposed as semantic universals? Fillmore states that his case relations correspond to "recognizable intrasentence relationships of the types discussed in studies of case systems (whether they are reflected in case affixes or not)," and are justified if they "can be shown to be comparable across languages" and "there is some predictive or explanatory use to which assumptions concerning the universality of these relations can be put."[13] I submit that there is nothing theoretically significant in the observation that there are recognizable intrasentence relationships that are comparable across languages, for this reflects nothing more than the truism noted at the outset of this section that all languages are capable of expressing a large body of common, universal experience. Therefore one will, of course, be able to find a good many such concepts, but this by itself does not endow them with any particular significance for semantic theory. Nor does the addition of the statement that there be some predictive or explanatory use to which these concepts can be put guarantee by any means that they will be theoretically justified, as experience with phonological theory has so often demonstrated. What all approaches to semantic theory of this kind suffer from is a failure to define semantic concepts on something other than the existential properties of the real world, which clearly lie outside of language. In other words, what all such approaches represent is a categorization of denotata rather than signata. If there is to be a linguistic semantics, we must be able to locate the ontological source of semantic concepts somewhere else than in the external world, and abstract claims to the effect that what we are really describing with such universals are the innate properties of the human mind are not satisfactory, since such claims are not in any way subject to verification.

Linguistic sign theory, on the other hand, does provide a solution to this critical problem. In sign theory semantic concepts are clearly defined on modes of perception, which are explicitly relatable both to extra-linguistic reality through the deictic process described above, and to linguistic reality by a direct correspondence to specific language forms. Thus the identification of semantic concepts in this theory satisfies the requirement that the ontological source of meaningful elements reside elsewhere than in the properties of the real world. But the individual signata thus identified are by definition language specific, so how does one arrive at a theory of semantic universals in such an approach? Actually, the same way as in phonology, and with very similar results.

A formally based theory of meaning necessarily proceeds in the direction from particulars to universals, from contextual variables to invariants at each successive level in the hierarchy of linguistic forms. In this process universals represent simply the highest, most abstract level of invariance in language. In his introduction to the most recent Festschrift in honor of Roman Jakobson, van Schooneveld described the hierarchy of invariance in language and the nature of the relationships that exist at each level.[14] At the first or lowest level we have to do with the analysis of the individual contextual usages of specific forms that comprise a particular grammatical or lexical category in a given language, and the determination of the invariant common denominator of meaning associated with each form. This first level of invariance may be called INTRACATEGORIAL INVARIANCE, and is the level, for example, at which Jakobson's analysis of the Russian case system is made. At the next higher level we investigate the properties held in common by the various grammatical and lexical categories within a given language. At this level, which may be called INTERCATEGORIAL INVARIANCE, the semantic properties determined for each of the categories individually are contextual variants, their differences being attributable to the nature of the category in which they occur. Thus, for example, in categories of grammatical meaning we see the features extracted all defined in terms of transmissional deixis, whereas in the verbal lexicon the same features recur in their perceptionally deictic variety. At the final level of invariance, which we may call INTERLINGUAL INVARIANCE,[15] the set of features that defines the overall semantic system of a particular language becomes once again a contextual variant in relation to the sets of features determined for other languages. The invariants at this final level are true semantic universals. Obviously these will be highly abstract concepts, and their precise nature remains for this reason extremely difficult to formulate. Nevertheless, enough progress has been made in this direction to suggest that a universal semantics comprises a uniquely linguistic form of algebra, some of the salient features of which are described below.

In Chapter 7 of the first volume of his *Semantic Transmutations*, van Schooneveld describes the nature of the hierarchy for Russian. He shows that the system is apparently governed by a single (though complex) perceptual operation that successively subdivides the universe of perception with each succeeding feature until the system eventually exhausts itself. The primitives in this system are nothing more than subsets of a perceptual universe created at each level in the hierarchy by successively restricting the conditions for perception until no further subset is conceivable. Let us look at how this system works, and as we do, bear in mind that what we are describing is not a hypothetical, deductive ordering of concepts, but a relationship among features, each of which has been defined individually on the observable formal categories of Russian, so that the extraordinary elegance and simplicity of the system is all the more remarkable. The order of features is as follows: transitivity, dimensionality, duplication, extension, restrictedness, objectivity.

In the beginning there is nothing but a perceptual universe with no identifiable features. The first feature in the hierarchy, **transitivity**,[16] creates the first set within this universe by singling out identifiable phenomena from the universe of perception. A transitive verb is distinct from an intransitive one in that the former requires, besides the subject, the presence of an object identified in the field of perception which the latter does not. Even when not expressed syntactically, the object is identifiable: cf. *ja čitaju* 'I am reading', where the subject has to be reading something. The second feature in the hierarchy, **dimensionality**, creates a subset from the preceding feature, giving the phenomenon referred to outlines or dimensions. Thus in verbal morphology, for example, the perfective aspect presents a phenomenon – in this case the verbal process – as a discrete one whose boundaries make it perceivable separately from any other verbal process, including specifically the speech event itself (see above, pages 152ff). In short dimensionality presents a phenomenon as distinct from all its peers. Dimensionality is also the feature that distinguishes, for example, Russian *v* 'in, into, to' from *na* 'in, into, to, on, onto': an object of the preposition *na* does not have to have any outlines, whereas the objects of *v* do. Dimensionality is also what distinguishes the preposition-preverbs *iz* and *vy-* from *ot* and *pere-* respectively, as we saw above (pages 80ff).

It is especially important to note that the formulation of the dimensionality feature presupposes the formulation of the transitivity feature in the hierarchy of features. In other words, the subset created by dimensionality is created from the set already established by transitivity through a further restriction of the conditions for perception. By the same token, the perceptual qualities specified by dimensionality are themselves prerequisites for the perception of the next feature in the hierarchy, duplication. **Duplication** requires that a phenomenon have outlines in order that a second phenomenon be able to be distinguished from it. Thus duplication presupposes dimensionality and then creates a second discrete phenomenon within the field of perception. In the Russian prepositional system the four prepositions *za* 'behind', *pered* 'in front of', *nad* 'over', and *pod* 'under' are all marked for duplication: the modified of the prepositional phrase in each of these cases requires the separate perception of the object of the preposition for its identification. With duplication, therefore, we have two separate phenomena within the field of vision.[17]

The next feature, **extension**, presupposes the existence of two phenomena and creates a relationship between them. In the case system of Russian, for example, the two phenomena in question are the speech event and the narrated event, and the extension feature creates the simplest form of marked case type, the accusative, where a relationship is established between the two. In the preposition-preverb system of Russian we noted that the forms *ot* and *iz* are distinguished from *vy-* and *pere-* respectively precisely by the presence in the former of a reference point which remains as a link between the narrated event and the situation that succeeds it (see above, page 87). Likewise, in the verbal lexicon of Russian we saw that determinate verbs of motion are marked for extension, since the final destination of the subject (or of the object if the verb is transitive) remains as a separate reference point linked to the speech situation (see above pages 107ff).

The fifth feature, **restrictedness**, presupposes the existence of a relationship between two phenomena and further narrows the field óf perception by cancelling this relationship. Recall that we described the grammatical category of tense as a whole as one in which a relationship between the narrated event and the speech event has been established – evident in the unmarked present tense – and we defined the preterite in particular as that tense form in which this relationship is specifically cancelled. In the category of case the unmarked case form – the nominative – merely establishes the narrated event and the speech event as two separate phenomena. The accusative then specifies a link between the two (i.e., is marked for extension), while the instrumental (marked for restrictedness) specifies that this link is cancelled, that is, that the phenomenon exists only in the situation described. Likewise the preposition-preverbs that we discussed at length in Chapter 3, all marked for restrictedness, presupposed an initial situation in which a relation between two phenomena had been established, and then cancelled this initial situation.

Finally, with the last feature in the hierarchy, **objectiveness**, the process of creating additional subsets in the field of perception exhausts itself. Objectivity (cf. the genitive case or the future tense as described above) specifies that the identification of a phenomenon is made only on the basis of its existence in the code. In other words, the system of subdividing the universe of perception, which began with the entire universe as its object, at this point turns in upon itself as the last possible source of identification. That the system apparently exhausts itself in this way by coming, as it were, to its own logical conclusion, strongly suggests that the features we are dealing with here, or at least something very close to these kinds of concepts, have validity beyond the single language in which they have been identified. This is not to say that these particular features are to be automatically granted the status of universals, but the very generality of the concepts they represent and the logical system they create makes it highly unlikely that there could be as many other differently structured logical systems as there are languages in the world. A much more likely possibility is that we will find a fairly large number of languages — those, perhaps, that are members of the same extended language family such as Slavic or maybe even Indoeuropean as a whole — whose semantic structures represent identifiable variants of one and the same basic system. At this point, however, our reasoning becomes largely speculative, so we must proceed with caution, but there are already indications that, at least in Slavic, the various languages may well operate off this one basic type (as we shall see in a moment below).

What is particularly intriguing about the way in which the hierarchy is evidently structured is that an identical logical operation seems to produce the next feature from the immediately preceding one at each level. Each new feature presupposes (anticipates, as it were) the field of perception already established by the preceding one, and then creates a new perceptual category by establishing a subset of the former. Van Schooneveld has labeled these two aspects of the process presupposition (anticipation) and subtraction respectively, and the fact that they define a single logical operation which is repeated at each level leads to the conclusion that the semantic structure of a given language may be governed by a single **semantic coefficient**.[18] This coefficient would differ from language to language, thus producing not entirely different features but feature systems that are largely comparable to one another. The problem of universal semantics would then become one of discovering what mechanism causes the shift in systems between languages, that is, of identifying the semantic coefficients of different languages.

To gain some insight into how the semantic coefficients of two closely related languages may be structured, we may consider the evidence from Serbocroatian in comparison with that of Russian. In an article written in 1967, van Schooneveld noted a semantic peculiarity that seems to recur in both the tense system and the system of prepositions in Serbocroatian.[19] In the tense system of Serbocroatian (as opposed to either Old Church Slavic or Old Russian) the aorist is a marked form which "introduces a **new** event in an already established past." That is, the use of an aorist in Serbocroatian presupposes the existence in the context of another past event. In a remarkably similar fashion, the prepositional system of Serbocroatian (as opposed to that of Russian) contains pairs of forms such as *iza* vs. *za* and *ispod* vs. *pod* where the difference appears to reside precisely in the fact that the forms with *iz-* (*is-*) contain a reference to an element already established in the context that is disallowed in the non-compound forms. Thus one cannot, for example, use the preposition *za* in the phrase *on stoji za stolom* 'he is standing behind the table' if the subject previously had a relationship to the table — e.g. was sitting there beforehand. In such a case only *iza stola* would occur, and would imply the previous establishment in the context of a relation to the table. This evidence suggests that Serbocroatian may possess a "semantic motif which pervades otherwise unrelated units of the morphological system" which is not present in Russian, namely a kind of deixis of the context.[20]

Taking this suggestion as a starting point, J. Levenberg has recently investigated the aspectual system of Serbocroatian, and has come up with strong confirmation of just such a "semantic motif."[21] Levenberg remarks, for example, on the inability of the Serbocroatian perfective non-past forms to indicate future time, which is the primary contextual variant of the Russian perfective non-past (see above, pp. 152ff). The Serbocroatian perfective necessarily indicates a process set off or delimited (dimensionality) from another process or event **in the context of the situation described.** From this and a variety of other evidence, including case usages, Levenberg concludes that we apparently have to do with the same sort of deixis of the context, distinguishing otherwise identical semantic features in Russian and Serbocroatian.

These observations are, of course, still preliminary in nature. We need to know much more before we can determine the mechanism behind a semantic coefficient (dominant) of the sort envisaged here, but one thing is certainly clear: that universal semantic relations represent a kind of linguistic calculus which itself is a form of set theory.

4. THE PLACE OF SYNTAX IN THE SIGN THEORY OF LANGUAGE

In Chapter 4 we made a series of observations intended to establish that the study of syntax lies just as much within the scope of a formally based semantic theory as does morphology. The subject matter of that chapter, however, was largely restricted to the phenomena of word order, with some additional consideration of verbal agreement and government. In this, the concluding section of the final chapter, I would like to make some further observations about syntactic structure and the place of syntax in the present theory. These remarks are themselves made possible by the preceding discussion of deixis, and demonstrate once again the crucial role that the concept of deixis plays in language.

At the outset of Chapter 4 we established that the study of syntax is not merely the analysis of the linear arrangement of forms, and that therefore syntactic phenomena are not satisfactorily explained by the construction of a purely formal mechanism capable of predicting their occurrence, no matter what ontological status we claim for such a formal mechanism. In other words, to say that the occurrence of two different syntactic configurations is "explained" by deriving them from two different deep structure configurations is not satisfactory unless there is an explicit way of assigning the relevant differential semantic properties directly to the deep structure configurations proposed. Unless this critical final step is taken, linguistic analysis remains in a vicious circle, merely relegating the difference between surface forms to a "deeper", more abstract level. This is not to say, however, that the determination of the formal relations themselves is irrelevant to linguistic analysis, and I would like to take special pains not to be misunderstood on this point. What I am saying is that such a step must not be taken as an end in itself, but should be seen as essentially heuristic; i.e., as a prerequisite to the determination of the semantic properties that correspond to the formal generalizations thus uncovered. This is because syntax is not merely an arrangement of forms, but rather an arrangement of meanings, which is reflected in the distribution of forms. Though it is true that in phonology and morphology the paradigmatic axis assumes the dominant role in determining informational content, whereas in syntax it is the syntagmatic axis which takes precedence, the switch from paradigmatic to syntagmatic predominance does not imply that semantic properties are therefore subordinated to formal properties in the domain of syntax. Rather, as with any change in hierarchical level in language, there is concomitant change in the **type** of semantic information present. There is, in fact, far less of a difference in this respect between syntax and morphology than there is between morphology and phonology. In the latter case (between phonology and morphology) there is a substantial difference in the kind of informational content present, since at the phonological level we find mere distinctiveness (negative informational content), while in morphology the forms do signify something. The kind of information present in morphology as opposed to syntax, however, actually varies from language to language, some languages expressing by morphological means what others express by syntactic configurations so that we must consider very carefully what type of information is carried by different languages at each of these two levels. Basically this information is of three kinds: lexical (including word-formative), grammatical, and stylistic; the latter two allowing expression either paradigmatically (i.e., morphologically) or syntagmatically. What this suggests it that the study of syntax cannot be conceived of as a strictly autonomous investigation because the kinds of information carried consistently by syntactic structures in all languages is relatively limited compared to the types of information signalled variously by either syntax or morphology depending on the language in question. We ought, therefore, as always, to be conscious of what formal means of expression are utilized in a particular language to convey what kinds of semantic information.

If there is one thing that does consistently define the realm of syntax as a **relatively** autonomous domain in all languages, however, it is that syntax remains the primary device for establishing reference. More than anything else, it is the syntagmatic concatenation of elements that determines the conditions for reference in a particular situation, since it is the insertion of a word in a syntagmatic context that produces a contextual meaning of a form. In other words, syntax is the primary vehicle by which specific denotata are created from signata. And the mechanism by which denotation is accomplished on the syntagmatic axis is, once again, deixis as we have now redefined it – i.e., as that property of meaning which allows a form to make reference to an identifiable, semelfactive act of perception.[22] Deixis is really nothing other than built-in reference, and it comes into full play in the domain of syntax, in the following manner. What deixis does in syntax is restrict the range of reference of a morpheme so that one can identify the referents of two or more elements (words) in a given syntactic string as belonging to the same act of perception. In other words, it is deixis that determines identity of reference on the syntagmatic axis, by establishing that two or more words with different signata will have the same denotatum. For example, if I say "green table", there is no reason why the denotata of 'green' and 'table' should be the same, except that once concatenated in a string on the syntagmatic axis, deixis once again comes into play and forces an identity of reference between the two denotata. Thus syntax is not so much even an arrangement of meanings as it is an obligatory merger of denotata, engendered by the syntagmatic operation of deixis.

Of course, the way in which deixis operates in syntax is complex and depends, among other things, upon the immediacy of the constituents involved and the peculiar deictic properties of individual lexical and grammatical morphemes. We can assume, however, that in a general sense syntactic relations consist of layers of modification relationships which have as their primary function the establishment (expression) of degrees of referential identity amongst the various constituents of a sentence. Rules of syntax are then rules for the identification of which denotata are to be perceived as merged in a particular situation. In the classic example 'old men and women', for instance, the rules of English syntax allow for two interpretations, one where the referent (denotatum) of 'old' merges with the referents of both nouns, and one where it merges with only the first of the two. The rules of English which govern these two interpretations are the result of the syntactic operation of perceptional deixis, which controls how we will perceive the merger of the referents in each case. We may conclude, therefore, that what underlies or determines the syntactic relationships involved in a sentence is a kind of hierarchical immediate constituent structure which **directly reflects the semantic relations amongst the constituents at each level** in the sentence. These semantic relations represent cues for interpreting the merger of denotata at each constituent level, beginning with the smallest constituents (or lowest level) and culminating in an interpretation of the sentence as a whole as making reference ultimately to a unified perception act. The ultimate unification of the perception act represented by the sentence is accomplished by the final (or highest level) modification relationship, the final merger of denotata, that where the subject is the ultimate modified of the sentence.

The model just sketched represents a general outline of how **intrasentence** relations of the type commonly handled by phrase structure rules would be treated in linguistic sign theory. I will assume for the purposes of the present discussion that the general framework given is adequate, and leave aside for the moment consideration of specific problems, which I intend to treat in a future volume devoted to syntax. The next question that needs to be addressed in this general discussion of principles concerns **intersentence** relations. We need to consider in particular whether a separate grammatical component is required to account for such relations, as is claimed, for example, in transformational theory, or whether, on the other hand, these phenomena are not also explainable in terms of the same specialized form of constituent analysis just described. I would like to suggest that no additional formal structures need to be created to account for intersentence relations, provided that we operate with a type of immediate constituent structure where semantic relations are inherent in the hierarchy of modification relationships itself. To test this assertion I propose that we consider one basic type of intersentence relation, that in which word order inversion produces questions from declarative sentences in a language such as English. To do this we will need to review for a moment the conclusions drawn in Chapter 4 concerning the semantic markings associated with English word order.

In Chapter 4 we observed that the marked word order in English is the one where the modifier follows the modified, and that the opposite word order is unmarked. Furthermore, we identified the semantic marking associated with post-position of the modifier in English as one which presents the modification relationship as being established uniquely in the given speech situation, and we called this marking deictic. We may now say, on the basis of the intervening discussion of deixis in this chapter, that the marking of post-posed modification in English is specifically a form of transmissional deixis which is superimposed upon the basic perceptional deixis that governs syntactic concatenation in general. The unmarked pre-posed modification type, by contrast, operates only with the latter type of deixis, the perceptional deixis inherent in syntagmatic concatenation itself. Reviewing briefly the evidence presented in Chapter 4, we may recall that post-posed adjectival and adverbial modification presents the modifier as one which describes its modified as it is presented in the given utterance situation. Thus, for example, in the sentence 'he painted the chair brown', the quality of 'brownness' is given to the chair in the particular situation, whereas in 'he painted the brown chair' the modification relationship is presented as having already been established before the utterance is made. Of particular importance to the present discussion is the observation that the normal word order for predication (as opposed to attribution) in English follows the marked syntactic type, and we may extend this observation to include not only predication by adjectival modification described in Chapter 4, but verbal predication as well. Thus just as a predicate adjective introduces a quality of the subject in the particular utterance situation, so, too, a verb attributes something to a subject in the specific utterance situation. In other words, predication – as represented by the normal declarative sentence type in English – presents the modification relationship as being established uniquely in the given situation. What makes a question different from a declarative statement is precisely the fact that we do not know when we question something whether the modification relationship has been established in the given situation or not. That is why we question it. And the unmarked word order – where the form that carries the main grammatical function of the verb (that is, the auxiliary or modal) precedes the subject – is exactly the one that makes no commitment in this respect. Hence inversion of subject and verb (of modified and modifier) is the normal word order for questions in English: cf. 'John is going' versus 'Is John going?'; 'John will go' versus 'Will John go?'; 'John should go' versus 'Should John go?'; 'John has gone' versus 'Has John gone?'; 'John did go' versus 'Did John go?'; and so forth.

It is particularly noteworthy that in English the inversion to the unmarked word order to create questions operates only with the auxiliary and modal forms of the verb, never with the lexical form (except in stylistically marked varieties of speech). The carrier of the lexical meaning stays put, and only the grammatical form moves to the unmarked position in front of the subject. Even when there is no autonomous grammatical form (modal or auxiliary) present in the declarative sentence type, one must be inserted to create a question in English: the simple present and past tenses both add forms of the auxiliary 'do' in such a case – cf. 'John went' versus 'Did John go?'; 'John goes' versus 'Does John go?'. Negation in English also requires the insertion of the auxiliary 'do': cf. 'John went' versus 'John did not go'; 'John goes' versus 'John does not go'.[23] In this context it is also significant that anaphoric reference to the verbal constituent of a sentence in English is regularly made by repeating only the grammatical form. Thus, for example, in so-called tag questions only the modal or auxiliary is repeated: cf. 'John is going, isn't he?'; 'John went, didn't he?'; 'John will go, won't he?'; and so forth. Cf. also 'Did you see John? No I didn't (Yes I did).'; 'Will you see John? No I won't (Yes I will).'; 'Are you going? No I'm not (Yes I am).'; 'Can you go? No I can't (Yes I can).'; etc.

I would suggest that all of these facts are semantically motivated and are engendered by the special transmissionally deictic marking of modification in English, which dominates the entire syntax of the language, and therefore affects the whole process by which reference is made in English. The transmissionally deictic marking of English modification is a peculiar feature of this language which makes it considerably different from, say, Russian or French. Recall that the analysis of modification in French and Russian presented above did not involve transmissional deixis, and in these languages, for example, pre-position of the lexical form of the verb is normal in the formulation of questions. It is significant that in English only that form of the verbal constituent may be pre-posed which is itself lexically marked for transmissional deixis, and it is this same form that is repeated in instances of anaphoric reference, and is inserted in cases of negation. The consistency with which the facts of English syntax revolve around the semantic presence of transmissionally deictic elements is simply too great to be ignored. Evidently the entire process of reference in English is colored by this form of deixis, which affects not only the semantically marked configurations, but the unmarked ones as well, since both members of a binary opposition reciprocally presuppose and imply each other. Just how the system works in detail, and how it differs from that of other languages, is of course a highly complex problem which will require a lengthy investigation, but the foundation for such an investigation is now firmly established, I believe, and its principles clearly stated.

Whatever the precise nature of the mechanism may be by which syntactic relationships are established, one thing seems clear: the positioning of elements in the surface structure of utterances is itself a direct reflection of the semantic properties of modification. It would appear, therefore, that the mechanism is indeed a semantic one, and that one and the same mechanism accounts for both intra- and inter- sentence regularities. Thus provided that we maintain the semantic integrity of formal elements in both morphology and syntax, we can begin to uncover the true generalities that underlie linguistic structure, the ultimate invariants in language. The overriding principle of language is to preserve one form for one meaning, and violations of this principle are tolerated only to a certain point before language does something to restore the balance. As Dwight Bolinger observes in his most enlightening recent work, *Meaning and Form*, the prevailing tendency to assume that *im*balance is the natural state of language is based upon a fallacy, which he attributes to "a confusion of competence and performance."[24] This confusion, he notes, produces assumptions of both false identity and false difference. On the one hand, the sameness that is commonly attributed to two different formal structures such as an active and a corresponding passive construction is in reality a performance variable, while the underlying difference between the two is what is codified in language. If you are asked 'What just happened?', you might answer either 'John slammed the door' or 'The door was slammed by John' with roughly equal probability. But if I ask 'What did John just do?' you are not going to answer 'The door was slammed by John.' In Bolinger's words,

The fact that a contrast that we carry in our competence is relevant does not mean that it is relevant all the time. It only means that it is there when we need it. If a language permits a contrast in form to survive, it ought to be for a purpose. When we look at what has happened historically to the accidental contrasts that have popped up, and the avidity with which speakers seize upon them to squeeze in a difference in meaning, come what may, we should form a proper appreciation of linguistic economy. It is not normal for language to waste its resources.[25]

Ultimately, the use of cognitive synonymy as a criterion for establishing sameness or difference in meaning must give way to a more linguistically sophisticated understanding of the role of meaning in language. The farther we cast our net in investigating the range of usage associated with individual formal categories, the more it becomes evident that synonymy and paraphrase relations – in short, all the transformations of one expression into another – are in fact the result of the accidental coalescence of referential properties and as such are potentially infinite in number and occurrence. The attempt to categorize such partial overlappings of meanings will necessarily result in a vicious relativity, which can be avoided only by maintaining a strict distinction between linguistic meaning and situational context.

We see the same fallacy repeated when false differences are attributed to the effect of purely contextual variables, which also properly belong to performance. Context may fool us into assigning separate senses to one and the same formal category when in fact, as we have observed throughout this book, the category in question simply remains neutral (unmarked) as to the various interpretations it may pick up in different situations. Bolinger's conclusion that failure to appreciate the semantic unity of the formal category in such cases amounts to assigning separate meanings to performance variables is one aspect of the larger problem which I have described as defining meaning on the existential properties of real-world situations rather than on the perceptual categories that actually underlie linguistic structure. That the latter really do provide the key to understanding language is proven by the fact that meaning encompasses much more than reports of events in the real world. Linguistic meaning, as Bolinger again notes, necessarily provides information about such things as what is central versus what is peripheral in a message, the speaker's perspective on the events he reports, and so forth.[26] And as often as not, fictitious and mistaken references constitute an essential part of linguistic messages. We may agree with Bolinger, and with William Haas whom he cites, that

The undoubted meaningfulness of fictions and of deceptive or mistaken references is in fact meaningfulness of the *most general* kind. It extends over all sentences. It is, on the contrary, the sense of the standard type of propositions that represents a more specific kind of meaningfulness: they fulfill the *additional* condition of true-or-false reference.[27]

An active and a corresponding passive construction may refer to the same external event or they may not because the formal categories of language are not in a one-to-one relation with existential situations. To conclude from this, however, that form and meaning are not in an isomorphic relationship to one another merely repeats the fallacy, for such a conclusion assumes an implicit equation of meaning with reference. Once we realize that meaning is properly defined on perceptual categories and not on referential situations, we can restore the fundamental isomorphism that provides the necessary economy of resources we must attribute to language, and ensures that our scientific description will be maximally general as well.

Precisely because syntactic phenomena straddle the boundary between competence and performance, we must be especially careful which aspects of syntax we assign to *langue* and which to *parole*. Clearly this is an empirical question, one which is all the more difficult to resolve given the fact that different languages assign differing roles to purely syntactic processes. Thus English, for example, expresses a substantial portion of its grammatical concepts by purely syntactic means, while a language like Russian utilizes primarily morphological processes to express grammatical relations.[28] Because such broad discrepancies from language to language exist in this respect, the integration of syntactic theory into general linguistic theory requires that we first distinguish carefully what formal means are utilized to express which kinds of concepts on a language to language basis. Only then can we begin to gauge which aspects of syntax properly belong to *langue* and which to *parole* — that is, to distinguish the truly general from the contextually determined elements in syntax. The theory outlined in this volume, with its systematic distinction between general and contextual meaning and its strict adherence to the principle of formal determinism, offers, I believe, the most promising approach to the solution of these problems. The analysis of syntactic phenomena is the focus of current research in linguistic sign theory which will be the subject of a companion volume to appear, hopefully, in the near future.

Notes

NOTES TO THE INTRODUCTION

1. For a discussion of the historical background of Jakobson's ideas, see my dissertation, *The Linguistic Thought of Roman Jakobson* (1970) and Elmar Holenstein, (1976), *Roman Jakobson's Approach to Language.*
2. R. Jakobson, "The Phonemic and Grammatical Aspects of Language in Their Interrelations," *SW II*, p. 103.
3. *Cours de linguistique générale*, p. 99.
4. *Op. cit.*, p. 103.
5. *Ibid.*, p. 104.
6. *Ibid.*, p. 105.
7. See, for example, Jakobson and Halle, (1956), *Fundamentals of Language.* The crucial question of the relative, rather than absolute, nature of phonological invariants is considered below in Chapter 1.
8. The determination of the *signata* in each case will differ from language to language.
9. *Op. cit.*, p. 103; bold type mine.
10. *Ibid.*, p. 104.
11. *Ibid.*
12. Of course, either the *signans* or the *signatum* may be zero, but such a zero is always a relational or functional zero.
13. L. Matejka, *Crossroads of Sound and Meaning*, p. 5.
14. "Implications of Language Universals for Linguistics," *SW II*, p. 586.

NOTES TO CHAPTER ONE

1. "The Kazan[i] School of Polish linguistics and its Place in the International Development of Phonology," *SW II*, pp. 394–428.
2. *Ibid.*, p. 394.
3. *Ibid.*, p. 395.
4. *Ibid.*, p. 395.
5. *Ibid.*, p. 396.

6. *Ibid.*, p. 418.
7. *Ibid.*
8. "Henry Sweet's Paths Towards Phonemics," *SW II*, p. 457.
9. "Linguistics in Relation to Other Sciences," *SW II*, p. 671.
10. "Henry Sweet's Paths Towards Phonemics," *SW II*, p. 457.
11. See especially his studies on aphasia and the relation of linguistics to other sciences in *Selected Writings*, Vol. II.
12. R. Jakobson and C.H. van Schooneveld, "Introductory Note." In M. Halle, (1959) *The Sound Pattern of Russian*, p. 6.
13. L. Matejka, "Crossroads of Sound and Meaning," p. 9.
14. R. Jakobson, "The Role of Phonic Elements in Speech Perception," *SW I*, p. 707. "The far-reaching difference between the sense-discriminating and sense-determining, formative devices must be carefully taken into account. . . So far as distinctive features are used in their purely discriminative function, possibilities of utilizing grammatical cues for their identification by the speech perceiver decrease to a minimum degree." *Ibid*, p. 710.
15. *Ibid.*, p. 706. Jakobson has stressed this point on a number of occasions. To the Symposium on the Structure of Language and its Mathematical Aspects, in 1960, he stated that:

    Language presents two considerably different aspects when seen from the two ends of the communication channel. Roughly, the encoding process goes from meaning to sound and from the lexico-grammatical to the phonological level, whereas the decoding process displays the opposite direction – from sound to meaning and from features to symbols. While a set (Einstellung) toward immediate constituents takes precedence in speech production, for speech perception the message is **first** a stochastic process. The probabilistic aspect of speech finds conspicious expression in the approach of the listener to homonyms, whereas for the speaker homonymy does not exist. When saying /sʌn/, he knows beforehand whether 'son' or 'sun' is meant, while the listener depends on the conditional probabilities of the context. [. . .]

    No doubt there is a feedback between speaking and hearing, but the hierarchy of the two processes is opposite for the encoder and decoder. These two aspects of language are irreducible to each other; both are equally essential and must be regarded as **complementary**. [. . .]

    Attempts to construct a model of language without any recourse to the speaker or the hearer, and thus to hypostasize a code detached from actual communication, threaten to make a scholastic fiction out of language.

    ["Linguistics and Communication Theory," *SW II*, pp. 575-6.].
16. "The Role of Phonic Elements in Speech Perception," *SW I*, p. 707.
17. *Ibid.*, pp. 714-5.
18. Bruce Derwing, *Transformational Grammar as a Theory of Language Acquisition*, p. 111.
19. C. Ferguson, Review of M. Halle, (1962), *Sound Pattern of Russian*. In *Language* 38 (3): 288.

20. See R. Jakobson, "Results of the Ninth International Congress of Linguists," *SW II*, p. 600.

21. "The Phonemic and Grammatical Aspects of Language in their Interrelations," *SW II*, pp. 114, 111.

22. "The Role of Phonic Elements in Speech Perception," *SW I*, p. 716. In view of the position being outlined here, one really must take exception to Morris Halle's recent interpretation of Jakobson's position, in which he maintains that Jakobson's own use of the distinction between these two levels "should be regarded as an expository device, and does not reflect the view that morphphonemics is a special level of representation distinct and separate from phonology." M. Halle, "Roman Jakobson's Contribution to the Modern Study of Speech Sounds." In L. Matejka, ed., (1976), *Sound, Sign and Meaning* (See especially pp. 94–5.) In fact, I believe that Jakobson's position is best described as intermediary between Halle's, in which no distinction between these two levels is made, and the view of those who would maintain a strict and total separation. I will elaborate further on this point below.

23. R. Jakobson, "Retrospect," *SW I*, p. 642.

24. See below, Chapter 3.

25. "Retrospect," *SW I*, pp. 641–2; bold type mine.

26. *Ibid.*; bold type and diagram supplied. The pertinent relations are enclosed in solid lines.

27. R. Jakobson, "On the Identification of Phonemic Entities," *SW I*, p. 424.

28. *Ibid.*, p. 423.

29. R. Jakobson, "The Role of Phonic Elements in Speech Perception," *SW I*, p. 712.

30. R. Jakobson, "Retrospect," *SW I*, p. 650.

31. R. Jakobson, "The Role of Phonic Elements in Speech Perception." *SW I*, p. 713. Jakobson addresses himself in this article to the full range of counterexamples commonly cited in discussions of autonomous phonemics. It is significant that this article is reprinted as the appendix to his most recent work in phonology: Jakobson and Waugh, (1979), *The Sound Shape of Language*. It is also significant that Jakobson's position on the issues under discussion here is reiterated in full force in this latest book.

32. *Ibid.*, p. 715.

33. *Ibid.*, pp. 710f.

34. R. Jakobson and L. Waugh, *The Sound Shape of Language*, p. 53.

35. R. Jakobson, "Efforts toward a Means-Ends Model of Language in Interwar Continental Linguistics," *SW II*, p. 523.

36. See *Ibid.*, *SW II*, pp. 522–6; and "The Concept of Sound Law and the Teleological Criterion." *SW I*, pp. 1–2. Whereas Chomsky, for example, views linguistics as a branch of cognitive psychology, Jakobson places linguistics within the general science of communication (semiotics). See "Language in Relation to Other Communication Systems," *SW II*, pp. 697–710; "Linguistics in Relation to Other Sciences," *SW II*, pp. 655–96; and *Main Trends in the Science of Language* (1974).

37. R. Jakobson, "The Concept of Sound Law and the Teleological Criterion," *SW I*, p. 2.

38. R. Jakobson, "The Role of Phonic Elements in Speech Perception," *SW I*, p. 715.
39. R. Jakobson, "Saussure's Unpublished Reflections on Phonemes," *SW I*, p. 747.
40. *Ibid.*, p. 746.
41. *Travaux du Cercle linguistique de Prague I*, 1929.
42. R. Jakobson and M. Halle, *Fundamentals of Language*, pp. 46–7.
43. R. Jakobson & L. Waugh, *The Sound Shape of Language*, pp. 60ff et passim.
44. "Extrapulmonic Consonants: Ejectives, Implosives, Clicks," *SW I*, pp. 720–7. See also *Fundamentals of Language*, p. 39f.
45. *Ibid.*, p. 726.
46. *Fundamentals of Language*, p. 49.

NOTES TO CHAPTER TWO

1. R. Jakobson, "The Phonemic and Grammatical Aspects of Language in their Interrelations," *SW II*, p. 110.
2. E. Sapir, *Language*, Chapter 4.
3. R. Jakobson and L. Waugh, *Op. cit.*, p. 55.
4. R. Jakobson, "The Role of Phonic Elements in Speech Perception," *SW I*, p. 710.
5. "The Phonemic and Grammatical Aspects. . .," *SW II*, p. 110.
6. "The Role of Phonic Elements. . .," *SW I*, p. 710.
7. "Zur Struktur des russischen Verbums," *SW II*, pp. 3–15.
   "Russian Conjugation," *SW II*, pp. 119–29.
   "Shifters, Verbal Categories, and the Russian Verb," *SW II*, pp. 130–47.
8. I use the term 'phonological' here and throughout this discussion in the neutral sense, not specifying whether the segments in question are phonemic or phonetic.
9. In the sense of Bloomfield, *Language*, § 13.4. Where Jakobson uses the terms 'phonemic' and 'morphophonemic' to describe alternations, Bloomfield utilizes the terms 'automatic' and 'grammatical' to make the same distinction. See "Russian Conjugation," *SW II*, p. 121.
10. I am indebted to C.H. van Schooneveld for singling this out as a critical point.
11. "The Phonemic and Grammatical Aspects. . .," *SW II*, p. 109.
12. See E. Stankiewicz, "Baudouin de Courtenay: His Life and Work." In Idem., *A Baudouin de Courtenay Anthology*, pp. 3–48.
    "Opposition and Hierarchy in Morphophonemic Alternations." In *To Honor Roman Jakobson*, pp. 1895–1905.
    "Prague School Morphophonemics." In L. Matejka, ed., *Sound, Sign, and Meaning*, pp. 101–19;
    and the general collection of his work on the subject, *Studies in Slavic Morphophonemics and Accentology*, 1979.
13. A. Reformatskij, *Iz istorii otečestvennoj fonoligii*, pp. 50–1.

14. In this last environment, velar consonants undergo BARE softening only before front vowels and SUBSTITUTIVE softening elsewhere because the sharpness feature is not distinctive in the velars. The one exception is the verb *tkat'*: /tku/, /tk'oš/, tkut/.
15. E. Stankiewicz, "Prague School Morphophonemics," p. 113.
16. See R. Jakobson, "Zur Struktur des russischen Verbums," and "Shifters,. . .".
17. *SW II*, pp. 154-83.
18. This material is revised from Jakobson's original study, "Beitrag zur allgemeinen Kasuslehre," which will be discussed in detail in Chapter 3 below.
19. *SW II*, pp. 148-53.
20. *Ibid.*, p. 153.
21. See in particular, "Quest for the Essence of Language," *SW II*, pp. 345-59, where the "isomorphic composition of signans and signatum" is subjected to a very revealing examination.
22. See, for example, "Linguistics and Poetics," in T. Sebeok, ed., *Style in Language*; and again, "The Phonemic and Grammatical Aspects of Language in their Interrelations," *SW II*, pp. 110-11: "The rhyme technique of diverse poets and poetic schools can be grammatical or antigrammatical, but it cannot be agrammatical. This means that the relation between the phonemic and grammatical structure of the rhyme always remains pertinent."

NOTES TO CHAPTER THREE

1. R. Jakobson, "Franz Boas' Approach to Language," *SW II*, p. 480.
2. "Notes on General Linguistics," pp. 36f.
3. "The Phonemic and Grammatical Aspects of Language in their Interrelations," *SW II*, p. 105.
4. "Boas' View of Grammatical Meaning," *SW II*, p. 493.
5. This discussion is cast in terms originally elaborated by Jakobson and further developed by E. Holenstein. I will return to this subject again in the final chapter where I will recast the discussion in the light of concepts presented in the interim. (See Chapter 5, Section 2.)
6. E. Holenstein, *Roman Jakobson's Approach to Language*, pp. 87f.
7. *Ibid.*, p. 88.
8. Recall that for some linguists, the assumption of the latter situation has been enough to provoke the conclusion that semantic structure lies outside the realm of linguistic reality entirely.
9. "On Linguistic Aspects of Translation," *SW II*, p. 260. See also, "Results of a Joint Conference of Anthropologists and Linguists," *SW II*, pp. 566f.
10. E. Holenstein, *Op. cit.*, p. 88.
11. R. Jakobson, "Linguistics and Communication Theory," *SW II*, pp. 573f.
12. E. Holenstein, *Op. cit.*, p. 88.
13. *Ibid.*
14. "Boas' View of Grammatical Meaning," *SW II*, pp. 494f.

15.   R. Jakobson, "Results of a Joint Conference of Anthropologists and Linguists," *SW II*, p. 564.
16.   See above, pp. 18f.
17.   "Linguistic Glosses to Goldstein's 'Wortbegriff'," *SW II*, p. 268.
18.   See especially, "Quest for the Essence of Language," *SW II*, pp. 345–59. Though symbol and sign are not, strictly speaking, interchangeable terms, what is said about a symbol here also holds for signs in general, if we allow for the moment that indexes and icons are specialized (marked) kinds of signs. (Cf. R. Jakobson, *Coup d'oeil sur le developpement de la sémiotique*, p. 8).
19.   R. Jakobson, "Pattern in Linguistics," *SW II*, p. 225. This article contains a series of observations about the nature of invariance both in linguistics and in other sciences as well.
20.   "Beitrag zur allgemeinen Kasuslehre," *SW II*, p. 24.
21.   *Ibid.*, p. 25.
22.   "Morfologičeskie nabljudenija...," *SW II*, p. 155.
23.   A.M. Peškovskij, *Russkij sintaksis v naučnom osveščenii* (6th edition, 1938), p. 274.
24.   *Ibid.*, pp. 57, 273–4. For similar comments to this effect about Peškovskij's analysis, see "Beitrag zur allgemeinen Kasuslehre," *SW II*, pp. 24f. and V.V. Vinogradov, *Russkij jazyk*, pp. 169ff.
25.   For him it is clear that the types of meanings noted above for the instrumental case are "perfectly well explained" by the single meaning of 'instrument', whereas other applications of the same case require the postulation of different meanings. See *Op. cit.*, pp. 274 and 282–4.
26.   The extent to which Jakobson's approach was influenced by Husserlian phenomenology and the extent to which it represents a phenomenology of language, has been studied rather thoroughly be E. Holenstein in his recent book. (See also my dissertation, *The Linguistic Thought of Roman Jakobson*, pp. 46ff.) Consequently I shall not go into the phenomenological aspect of Jakobson's work here, but will have occasion later to remark on the extent of his contributions to the theory of phenomenology.
27.   For more on the relation of Jakobson's work to mathematical theories of invariance, see E. Holenstein, *Op. cit.*, pp. 21ff.
28.   E. Holenstein, *Op. cit.*, pp. 16–7. Bold type added.
29.   Another example from outside linguistics: "In W. Kohler's experiment, chickens were trained to pick grain from a gray field and to leave the grain untouched on the adjacent, darker field; when the pair of fields, gray and dark, was later replaced by a pair, gray and light, the chickens looking for their food left the gray field for its lighter counterpart. Thus 'the chicken transfers its response to the relatively brighter area.'" ("Phonology and Phonetics," *SW I*, p. 473.) For still further evidence on perceptual invariance, see "The Role of Phonic Elements...," *SW I*, pp. 707–8.
30.   "Morfologičeskie nabljudenija...," *SW II*, pp. 155f.
31.   *Ibid.*, p. 156.
32.   *Ibid.*, p. 157. For a more detailed analysis of the general meaning of the G case, see "Beitrag zur allgemeinen Kasuslehre," *SW II*, pp. 37ff.

33. H.J. Pos, (1938), "La notion d'opposition en linguistique," *XI Congrès international de psychologie*, p. 245.
34. The features identified here will be defined and illustrated in various places throughout this text.
35. E. Holenstein, *Op. cit.*, pp. 82f.
36. It is largely for this reason that Jakobson prefers to restrict the use of the term *distinctive* feature to refer only to phonological oppositions. At the level of meaning he speaks of *semantic* or *conceptual* features. See, e.g., "Verbal Communication," *Scientific American*, September, 1972, pp. 72ff.
37. "Morfologičeskie nabljudenija. . .," p. 159.
38. Significantly, if one wanted to say that a whole piece of chalk was used up, the Russian expression would be *ispol'zovat' melok*, where the object is again in the A case.
39. R. Jakobson, "Implications of Language Universals for Linguistics," *SW II*, p. 587.
40. *Ibid.*
41. "Zur Struktur des russischen Verbums," *SW II*, p. 3; reiterated in "Beitrag zur allgemeinen Kasuslehre," *SW II*, pp. 29f.
42. "The Relation between Genitive and Plural in the Declension of Russian Nouns," *SW II*, p. 148.
43. See above, p. 60.
44. See "Zur Struktur des russischen Verbums," *SW II*, p. 4.
45. R. Jakobson, "Verbal Communication." In *Scientific American* 227: 77. Though made with reference to the properties of sounds, this statement holds true for semantic relations as well.
46. See above, page 69. See also E. Holenstein, *Op. cit.*, p. 132, and Jakobson, "Zur Struktur des russischen Verbums," *SW II*, p. 4.
47. E. Holenstein, *Op. cit.*, p. 131.
48. L. Waugh, *Roman Jakobson's Science of Language*, p. 92.
49. See L. Waugh, *op. cit.*, p. 95.
50. See E. Holenstein, *Roman Jakobson's Approach to Language*, p. 131.
51. See E. Holenstein, *Op. cit.*, p. 135.
52. "Beitrag zur allgemeinen Kasuslehre," *SW II*, p. 49.
53. E. Holenstein, *Op. cit.*, p. 134.
54. C.H. van Schooneveld, "By Way of Introduction: Roman Jakobson's Tenets and their Potential." In D. Armstrong and C.H. van Schooneveld, eds., *Roman Jakobson: Echoes of his Scholarship*, pp. 3ff.
55. C.H. van Schooneveld, (1978), *Semantic Transmutations*. The apparent similarity between the three features of the preposition/preverb system, extension, restrictedness and objectiveness, on the one hand, and the three features directionality, marginality and quantification constituting the case system on the other, lead van Schooneveld to the hypothesis that their obvious differences might be due to the operation of the first group within the category of preposition/preverb, and the operation of the second group within the category of case. The reformulation of Jakobson's case features ultimately lead to the conclusion that the apparent similarity is in fact an identity.
56. C.H. van Schooneveld, *Semantic Transmutations*, pp. 48, 64, 86f.

57. *Semantic Transmutations*, pp. 36ff, 123ff.
58. Note that the meaning of cancellation of a relationship to a point is quite different from what happens, for example, with the preposition *v* 'in, into', where instead of cancelling a relationship, the process obviously establishes one.
59. *Semantic Transmutations*, pp. 137ff.
60. *Semantic Transmutations*, pp. 142ff.
61. Both are also marked for extension in van Schooneveld's system. That *ot* is unmarked for dimensionality explains why the source of *ot* may sometimes be ambiguous with respect to having or not having dimensions (see the discussion above on the meaning of unmarked categories). For more on the dimensionality feature in this context, see immediately below. pp. 92f.
62. This example is doubly interesting because of the use of the word 'over', which in English combines the connotations of completion (or cancellation of the process) and movement across to the other side of, both of which are also combined in the feature of restrictedness, as we shall see when we consider the Russian preverb *pere-* below.
63. *Semantic Transmutations*, pp. 146f.
64. C.H. van Schooneveld, (1978), "Contribution à l'étude comparative des systèmes des cas, des prépositions et des catégories grammaticales du verbe en russe moderne." In *Slavica Hierosolymitana* 2: 44ff.
65. The choice of tense and aspect here is not in any way prejudicial, since the function of the accusative remains the same whether the process has actually been completed or, for that matter, not yet even begun. All that changes with tense and aspect is the relative perspective of the addressee vis-à-vis the verb.
66. R. Jakobson, "Beitrag zur allgemeinen Kasuslehre," *SW II*, p. 48.
67. Not all the meanings of the prepositions have yet been established, but the analysis of the basic ones is now more or less complete. We have considered only some of the features and a few of the prepositions in this study. For the complete analysis, see *Semantic Transmutations*.
68. The concept of deixis and its implications for linguistic analysis are fully elaborated upon in Chapter 5.
69. See C.H. van Schooneveld, "Roman Jakouson's Tenets and their Potential," pp. 5f.
70. C.H. van Schooneveld, "The Extension Feature in Russian." In *Festschrift for E. Stankiewicz* (forthcoming).
71. A most interesting and important problem yet to be worked out is what distinguishes the meaning of a form like *minovat'* from one like *otbyt'*, which we saw above in the discussion of the prefix *ot*. Both verbs add the markings of restrictedness to the basic meaning 'be', but the former does it lexically with the resulting meaning of 'pass', while the latter operates with word formation and the resulting meaning is 'serve time' (see above, page 86). Just how these different operations affect the meaning of a form is a central issue for future research.
72. C.H. van Schooneveld, "Roman Jakobson's Tenets. . .," pp. 5f.

NOTES TO CHAPTER FOUR

1. Significantly, this type of phrasal modification does not require post-position in Russian.
2. D.L. Bolinger, (1952), "Linear Modification." *PMLA* 67: 1117–44. Reprinted in Householder (ed.), *Syntactic Theory I*: 31–50.
3. *Ibid.*, p. 43 (in the reprinted edition).
4. D.E. Rozental', *Praktičeskaja stilistika russkogo jazyka*, p. 232.
5. A.A. Šaxmatov, *Sintaksis russkogo jazyka*, p. 292.
6. C.H. van Schooneveld, "On the Word Order in Modern Russian." *IJSLP* 3: 41.
7. *Ibid.*, p. 43.
8. E. Holenstein, *Op. cit.*, pp. 109f.
9. See C.H. van Schooneveld, (1964), "On Word Order In Modern Russian," and "Zur vergleichenden sematischen Struktur der Wortfolge in der russischen, deutschen, französischen und englischen Sprache,: *Wiener Slavistisches Jahrbuch* II: pp. 94–100. See also "Roman Jakobson's Tenets. . .," p. 10. The quotations in the following paragraph are from the first reference.
10. Bolinger, *Op. cit.*
11. M. Grevisse, *Le bon usage*, 9th edition, p. 338.
12. Most of the examples in this section are taken from R. Sangster and L. Waugh "The Semantics of Syntax: A Semantic Investigation of Adjective Placemen in French." For a more elaborate treatment of the French adjective from this point of view, see L. Waugh, *A Semantic Analysis of Word Order: Adjective Position in French*. Leiden: E.J. Brill, 1977. See also L. Waugh, (1976), "The Semantics and Paradigmatics of Word Order," *Language 52*.
13. That such adjectives may occasionally also occur in post-position with a metaphorical connotation (*bête noire, misère noire*, etc.) should not surprise us, since such types merely reflect the ambiguity inherent in the unmarked member of any semantic opposition.

NOTES TO CHAPTER FIVE

1. U. Weinreich, "Explorations in Semantic Theory." In T. Sebeok, ed., *Current Trends in Linguistics III*: p. 469.
2. As formulated in the previous century by M. Kruszewski, "Words . . . differ from each other not only in terms of their meaning, but also in their outward form. . . Here we can make a first approximation to a law of the development of language: the law of relationship of the sphere of words to the sphere of thought. Indeed, if language is nothing other than a system of signs, then the ideal state of language would be that in which, between the system of signs and that which they signify, there is a complete correlation. . . The development of language is an eternal striving towards this ideal." *Očerk nauki o jazyke*. Kazan', 1883. § 39.
3. R. Jakobson, "The Role of Phonic Elements. . .," *SW I*, p. 707.
4. R. Jakobson, "Beitrag. . .," p. 31.

5. *Ibid.*, p. 54.
6. C.H. van Schooneveld, "Contribution à l'étude comparative. . .," pp. 48f.
7. See above, pp. 91ff.
8. See, for example, J. Forsyth, *A Grammar of Aspect*, sections 6.5.1 through 6.5.4 et passim.
9. Cf. R. Jakobson, "Shifters, Verbal Categories and the Russian Verb."
10. See, for example, J. Ferrell, "On the Aspects of *byt'* and on the Position of the Periphrastic Imperative Future in Contemporary Literary Russian," *Word 9*: 362–76.
11. "Roman Jakobson's Tenets. . .," p. 5.
12. C.J. Fillmore, "The Case for Case," in Bach and Harms, eds., *Universals in Linguistic Theory*, p. 32.
13. *Ibid.*, p. 20.
14. "Roman Jakobson's Tenets. . .," pp. 1ff.
15. See also R. Jakobson, "Implications of Language Universals for Linguistics," *SW II*, p. 581.
16. For a more detailed treatment of the transitivity feature, see C.H. van Schooneveld, "A Semantic Proteus: The Transitivity Feature in Russian," In *Ezikovedski proučvanija v čest na akad. V.I. Georgiev*, Sofia, 1980, pp. 377–85.
17. See *Semantic Transmutations*, pp. 77–95 and 173–185.
18. *Semantic Transmutations*, Chapters 1 and 7. Current discussions favor changing this term to *semantic dominant* to avoid confusion with the use of the term in mathematics.
19. "On the Meaning of the Serbocroatian Aorist." In *To Honor Roman Jakobson*, pp. 2126–9.
20. *Ibid.*, pp. 2128–9.
21. Joel Levenberg, *A Semantic Analysis of Verbal Aspect in Russian and Serbocroatian*, Indiana University Ph.D. Dissertation, 1980.
22. The formulation of the role of deixis presented in this paragraph is elaborated from C.H. van Schooneveld, "Roman Jakobson's Tenets. . .," pp. 8–9.
23. Another, perhaps preferable, way of analyzing the relationship between these constructions involving the simple present and the past tenses is to treat the difference between, e.g., 'John went' versus 'John did go' on the one hand, and 'John goes' versus 'John does go' on the other, as being neutralized under questioning and negation, since only the type with the auxiliary occurs under these conditions. This is because apparently only the specific occurrence of a situation can be questioned or negated in English, that is, only the transmissionally deictic stipulation of its existence undergoes questioning and negation. In any event, a semantically sensitive syntactic analysis requires that we do **not** treat the absence of the auxiliary as an instance of deletion (cf. the "do drop" rule in TG), for such a rule makes a semantically unacceptable claim: that there is no difference in meaning between the constructions with and without 'do', or that 'do' itself has no meaning in such cases. The existence of a deletion rule here can only be justified on purely formal grounds; i.e., that deletion of 'do' produces a "simpler" explanation of the purely formal structures observed.
24. D. Bolinger, *Meaning and Form*, p. 18.

25. *Ibid.*, pp. 18-9.
26. *Ibid.*, p. 4. Note the closeness of these concepts to the types of features proposed in this study.
27. W. Haas, (1975), "Syntax and Semantics in Ordinary Language," *Aristotelian Society Supplementary Volume 49*: 158-9. [Italics in the original.]
28. It might well be (though this is a purely speculative judgment at this time) that the peculiarly deictic marking of English modification relationships discussed above accounts in some sense for the syntactic expression of grammatical relations in English, grammatical categories being marked for transmissional deixis.

Bibliography

This bibliography includes references to a number of works not specifically cited in the text which adhere more or less directly to the principles put forth in this study. The authors of such works are identified by an asterisk. I have listed all the items in van Schooneveld's bibliography which pertain to the development of linguistic sign theory. The references given for Jakobson, on the other hand, are just those actually cited in the text. No attempt has been made to present his bibliography any more extensively, since a number of thorough listings have already appeared in print. Jakobson's works are presented here according to their original place and date of publication, whereas in the notes throughout the text, those articles that have been reprinted in his *Selected Writings* (*SW I* and *SW II*) are cited according to the reprinted versions. In this manner I have attempted to combine a measure of historical information in the bibliography with ease of reference to quotations in the text. Finally, in order to keep the titles of cited articles before the reader at all times, I have keyed both the bibliography and the notes to titles rather than to dates of publication. Thus multiple works of a single author are listed here in alphabetical order by title.

*Armstrong, J. Daniel (1973). *A Semantic Approach to Russian Word Formation: Suffixal Word Formation in Substantives*. Indiana University Ph.D. dissertaton.
— (1978). "Toward a Comparative Semantic Analysis of Suffixal Word Formation in Slavic." In H. Birnbaum, ed., *American Contributions to the Eighth International Congress of Slavists, I: Linguistics and Poetics*. Columbus OH: Slavica.
Bloomfield, Leonard (1933). *Language*. New York: Henry Holt.

Bolinger, Dwight L. (1967). "Adjectives in English: Attribution and Predication." *Lingua* 18; 1-34.

— (1952). "Linear Modification." *PMLA* 67: 1117-1144.

— (1977). *Meaning and Form*. London: Longman.

*Bouma, Lowell (1975). "On Contrasting the Semantics of the Modal
Auxiliaries of German and English." *Lingua* 37: 313-339.

Chomsky, Noam (1964). *Current Issues in Linguistic Theory*. The Hague:
Mouton.

— (1972). *Language and Mind*. Enlarged ed. New York: Harcourt.

Cook, Walter A., S.J. (1979). *Case Grammar: Development of the Matrix
Model. 1970-1978*. Washington, D.C.: Georgetown U. P.

Derwing, Bruce (1973). *Transformational Grammar as a Theory of Language Acquisition*. Cambridge: Cambridge U. P.

Fillmore, Charles J. (1968). "The Case for Case." In Bach and Harms, eds.,
Universals in Linguistic Theory. New York: Holt.

— (1977). "The Case for Case Reopened." In P. Cole and J. Sadok, eds.,
Syntax and Semantics, Vol. 8: Grammatical Relations. New York:
Academic Press.

— (1975). *Principles of Case Grammar: The Structure of Language and
Meaning*. Tokyo: Sanseido.

*Gardiner, Duncan B. (1979). "On the Notion 'Structural Semantics'."
Paper read before the University of Kentucky Linguistic Circle,
March 1979.

— "Prague School Semantics Today." To appear in the Festschrift in memory of J. Daniel Armstrong. Columbus OH: Slavica.

— (1979). "The Semantics of Russian Verbal Suffixes: A First Look."
SEEJ 23: 381-394.

Ferguson, Charles (1962). Review of M. Halle, *The Sound Pattern of
Russian. Language* 38 (3).

Ferrell, J. (1953). "On the Aspects of *byt'* and the Position of the Periphrastic Imperfective in Contemporary Literary Russian." *Word* 9:
362-376.

Forsyth, J. (1970). *A Grammar of Aspect: Usage and Meaning in the
Russian Verb*. Cambridge: Cambridge U. P.

Grevisse, Maurice (1969). *Le bon usage: grammaire française*. 9th ed.
Gembloux: Editions J. Duculot.

Haas, W. (1975). "Syntax and Semantics in Ordinary Language." *Aristotelian
Society Supplementary Volume* 49: 158-9.

Halle, Morris (1976). "Roman Jakobson's Contribution to the Modern

Study of Speech Sounds." In L. Matejka, ed., *Sound, Sign and Meaning*. Ann Arbor: Michigan Slavic Contributions.
— (1959). *The Sound Pattern of Russian*. The Hague: Mouton.
*Holenstein, Elmar (1976). *Roman Jakobson's Approach to Language: Phenomenological Structuralism*. Bloomington: Indiana U. P.
*Howden, Marcia (1979). "Structure in the Lexicon: The French Adjectives *Neuf* and *Nouveau*." In L. Waugh and F. van Coetsem, eds., *Cornell Linguistic Contributions, II: Contributions to Grammatical Studies*. Leiden: E.J. Brill.
*Jakobson, Roman (1936). "Beitrag zur allgemeinen Kasuslehre." *TCLP* 6.
— (1971). *A Bibliography of his Writings*. The Hague: Mouton.
— "Boas' View of Grammatical Meaning." *The Anthropology of Franz Boas*. (American Anthropology Association Memoir LXXX.)
— (1928). "The Concept of Sound Law and the Teleological Criterion." *Časopis pro moderní filologii*. Prague.
— (1975). *Coup d'oeil sur le développement de la sémiotique*. (Studies in Semiotics, Vol. 3.) Bloomington: Indiana U. Publications.
— (1963). "Efforts towards a Means-Ends Model of Language in Interwar Continental Linguistics." In C. Mohrmann, ed., *Trends in Modern Linguistics*. Utrecht: Spectrum.
— (1969). "Extrapulmonic Consonants: Ejectives, Implosives, Clicks." *To Honour George Akhvlediani*. Tbilisi University. Also published in *Quarterly Progress Report of the Research Laboratory of Electronics at MIT* LXC: 221-7.
— (1944). "Franz Boas' Approach to Language." *IJAL* 10.
— (1966). "Henry Sweet's Paths towards Phonemics." In C.E. Bazell, ed., *In Memory of J.R. Firth*. London: Longman.
— (1963). "Implications of Language Universals for Linguistics." In J. Greenberg, ed., *Universals of Language*. Cambridge: MIT Press.
— (1958). "The Kazan' School of Polish Linguistics and its Place in the International Development of Phonology." Based on a paper given at a meeting of the Linguistic Committee of the Polish Academy of Sciences in Warsaw, January 1958.
— (1968). "Language in Relation to Other Communication Systems." Lecture delivered at the International Symposium "Languages in Society and in Technique" in Milan, October 1968.
— (1959). "Linguistic Glosses to Goldstein's 'Wortbegriff'." *Journal of Individual Psychology* 15.
— (1961). "Linguistics and Communication Theory." *Proceedings of Symposia in Applied Mathematics* 12.

198   Bibliography

– (1960). "Linguistics and Poetics." In T. Sebeok, ed., *Style in Language*. Cambridge: MIT Press.

– (1970). "Linguistics in Relation to Other Sciences." Originally written as part of a survey on linguistics for the Unesco publication *Main Trends of Research in the Social and Human Sciences*.

– (1973). *Main Trends in the Science of Language*. New York: Harper and Row.

– (1958). "Morfologičeskie nabljudenija nad slavjanskim skloneniem." *American Contributions to the Fourth International Congress of Slavists*. The Hague: Mouton.

– (1949). *Notes on General Linguistics: Its Present State and Crucial Problems*. New York: Rockefeller Foundation. Mimeo.

– (1959) "On Linguistic Aspects of Translation." *On Translation*. Cambridge: Harvard U. P.

– (1949). "On the Identification of Phonemic Entities." *Travaux du Cercle Linguistique de Copenhague* 5.

– (1952). "Pattern in Linguistics." Statement made at the International Symposium on Anthropology (New York, June 1952).

– (1949). "The Phonemic and Grammatical Aspects of Language in their Interrelations." *Actes du Sixième Congrès International des Linguistes*. Paris: Juillet.

– (1965). "Quest for the Essence of Language." Address to the American Academy of Arts and Sciences, February 1965.

– (1957). "The Relation between Genitive and Plural in the Declension of Russian Nouns." *Scando-Slavica* 3.

– (1953). "Results of a Joint Conference of Anthropologists and Linguists." *IJAL* 19.

– (1962). "Results of the Ninth International Congress of Linguists." Concluding address to the Congress (Cambridge, Mass., August 1962).

– (1971). "Retrospect." *Selected Writings, I: Phonological Studies*, pp. 631–658. The Hague: Mouton.

– (1968). "The Role of Phonic Elements in Speech Perception." *Zeitschrift für Phonetik, Sprachwissenschaft und Kommunikationsforschung* 21. Also reprinted in R. Jakobson and L. Waugh, *The Sound Shape of Language*.

– (1948). "Russian Conjugation." *Word* 4.

– (1970). "Saussure's Unpublished Reflections on Phonemes." *Cahiers F. de Saussure* 26.

– (1971). *Selected Writings, I: Phonological Studies*. Second expanded ed. The Hague: Mouton.

— (1971). *Selected Writings, II: Word and Language*. The Hague: Mouton.
— (1957). "Shifters, Verbal Categories and the Russian Verb." Published by the Harvard University Department of Slavic Languages and Literatures.
— (1972). "Verbal Communication." *Scientific American* 227 (September).
— (1932). "Zur Struktur des russischen Verbums." *Charisteria Gvilelmo Mathesio...oblata*. Prague.
Jakobson, Roman and Morris Halle (1956). *Fundamentals of Language*. The Hague: Mouton.
— (1957). "Phonology and Phonetics." In L. Kaiser, ed., *Manual of Phonetics*. Amsterdam: North Holland Publishing Company.
Jakobson, Roman and C.H. van Schooneveld (1959). "Introductory Note." In M. Halle, *The Sound Pattern of Russian*. The Hague: Mouton.
Jakobson, Roman and Linda R. Waugh (1979). *The Sound Shape of Language*. Bloomington: Indiana U. P.
Johnson, D. Barton (1970). *Transformations and their Use in the Resolution of Syntactic Homomorphy*. The Hague: Mouton.
Kruszewski, M. (1883). *Očerk nauki o jazyke*. Kazan'.
*Levenberg, Joel (1980). *A Semantic Analysis of Verbal Aspect in Russian and Serbo-Croatian*. Indiana University Ph.D. dissertation.
Lyons, John (1977). *Semantics*. 2 vols. Cambridge: Cambridge U. P.
*Matejka, Ladislav (1975). *Crossroads of Sound and Meaning*. Lisse: P. de Ridder Press.
— (1976). (ed.) *Sound, Sign and Meaning: Quinquagenary of the Prague Linguistic Circle*. Ann Arbor: Michigan Slavic Contributions 6.
Peškovskij, A.M. (1938). *Russkij Sintaksis v naučnom osveščenii*. 6th ed. Moscow: Gos. učeb. -pedagog. izd-vo.
Pos, H.J. (1938). "La notion d'opposition en linguistique." *XI Congrès international de psychologie*. Paris: Alcan.
Reformatskij, A.A. (1970). *Iz istorii otečestvennoj fonologii*. Moscow: Nauka.
Rozenthal', D.E. (1968). *Praktičeskaja stilistika russkogo jazyka*. 2nd ed. Moscow: Iskusstvo.
*Sangster, Rodney B. (1970). *The Linguistic Thought of Roman Jakobson*. Indiana University Ph.D. dissertation.
*Sangster, Rodney B. and Linda R. Waugh (1978). "The Semantics of Syntax: A Semantic Investigation of Adjective Placement in French." In V. Honsa and M. Hardman de Bautista, eds., *Papers on Linguistics and Child Language*. The Hague: Mouton.
Sapir, Edward (1921). *Language*. New York: Harcourt, Brace.

Saussure, Ferdinand de (1955). *Cours de linguistique générale*. 3rd ed. Paris: Payot.

*Stankiewicz, Edward (1972). "Baudouin de Courtenay: His Life and Work." In E. Stankiewicz, ed., *A Baudouin de Courtenay Anthology*. Bloomington: Indiana U. P.

— (1969). "Opposition and Hierarchy in Morphophonemic Alternations." In *To Honor Roman Jakobson*. The Hague: Mouton.

— (1976). "Prague School Morphophonemics." In E. Matejka, ed., *Sound, Sign and Meaning*. Ann Arbor: Michigan Slavic Contributions.

— (1979). *Studies in Slavic Morphophonemics and Accentology*. Ann Arbor: Michigan Slavic Publications.

Steiner, George (1975). *After Babel: Aspects of Language and Translation*. London: Oxford U. P.

Šaxmatov, A.A. (1941). *Sintaksis russkogo jazyka*. 2nd ed. Leningrad: AN-SSSR.

Travaux du Cercle linguistique de Prague, 1 (1929).

*van Schooneveld, C.H. (1963). "Allomorph versus Morpheme in Contemporary Standard Russian." *American Contributions to the Fifth International Congress of Slavists*, Vol. 1. The Hague: Mouton.

— (1977). "By Way of Introduction: Roman Jakobson's Tenets and their Potential." In D. Armstrong and C.H. van Schooneveld, eds., *Roman Jakobson: Echoes of his Scholarship*. Lisse: P. de Ridder Press.

— (1978). "Contribution à l'étude comparative des systèmes des cas, des prépositions et des catégories grammaticales du verbe en russe moderne." *Studia Slavica Hierosolymitana* 2: 41-50.

— "The Extension Feature in Russian." To appear in the Festschrift for Edward Stankiewicz.

— (1973). "The Morphemic Structure of the Slavic Word and Greenberg's 28th Universal." *Slavic Word*. The Hague: Mouton.

— (1978). "Neogrammarian Sound Law and Syntagmatic Structure." In V. Honsa and M. Hardman de Bautista, eds., *Papers on Linguistics and Child Language*. The Hague: Mouton.

— (1967). "On The Meaning of the Serbo-Croatian Aorist." *To Honor Roman Jakobson*, Vol. 3. The Hague: Mouton.

— (1968). "On the Opposition Determinate–Indeterminate in the Contemporary Standard Russian Verb." *American Contributions to the Sixth International Congress of Slavists, Vol. 1*. The Hague: Mouton.

— (1960). "On the Word Order in Modern Russian." *IJSLP* 3: 40-44.

— (1977). "The Place of Gender in the Semantic Structure of the Russian Language." *Scando-Slavica* 23: 129-138.

– (1959). *A Semantic Analysis of the Old Russian Finite Preterite System.* The Hague: Mouton.

– (1978). "A Semantic Approach to the Analysis of Word Formation in Contemporary Standard Russian." *American Contributions to the Eighth International Congress of Slavists, I: Linguistics and Poetics.* Columbus OH: Slavica.

– (1980). "A Semantic Proteus: The Transitivity Feature in Russian." *Ezikovedski proučvanija v čest na akad. V.I. Georgiev.* Sofia: Bălgarska Akademia na Naukite.

– (1978). *Semantic Transmutations: Prolegomena to a Calculus of Meaning, I: The Cardinal Semantic Structure of the Prepositions, Cases, and Paratactic Conjunctions in Contemporary Standard Russian.* Bloomington: Physsardt.

– (1958). "The So-called 'préverbes vides' and Neutralization." *Dutch Contributions to the Fourth International Congress of Slavists.* The Hague: Mouton.

– (1964). "Zur vergleichenden semantischen Struktur der Wortfolge in der russischen, deutschen, französischen und englischen Sprache." *Wiener Slavistisches Jahrbuch* 11: 94–100.

*van Schooneveld, C.H. and J.E. Buning-Jurgens (1961). *The Sentence Intonation of Contemporary Standard Russian as a Linguistic Structure.* The Hague: Mouton.

Vinogradov, V.V. (1947). *Russkij jazyk.* Moscow: Gos. učeb. -pedagog. izd-vo.

*Waugh, Linda R. (1978). "The Context-Sensitive Meaning of the French Subjunctive." *Contributions to Grammatical Studies: Semantics and Syntax.* Leiden: Brill.

– (1976). "Lexical Meaning: The Prepositions *en* and *dans* in French." *Lingua* 39: 69–118.

– "Marked and Unmarked: A Choice between Unequals in Semiotic Structure." To appear in *Semiotica.*

– (1979). "Markedness and Phonological Systems." *LACUS* V. Columbia, S. C.: Hornbeam Press.

– (1979). "Remarks on Markedness." In D. Dinnsen, ed., *Current Approaches to Phonological Theory.* Bloomington: Indiana U. P.

– (1976). *Roman Jakobson's Science of Language.* Lisse: P. de Ridder Press.

– (1975). "A Semantic Analysis of the French Tense System." *Orbis* 24: 436–485.

– (1977). *A Semantic Analysis of Word Order: Adjective Position in French.* Leiden: E.J. Brill.

– (1976). "The Semantics and Paradigmatics of Word Order." *Language* 52: 82-107.

Weinreich, Uriel (1966). "Explorations in Semantic Theory." In T. Sebeok, ed., *Current Trends in Linguistics* 3. The Hague: Mouton.

Index

Abstractness
   In phonology ix, 22
   Of conceptual features 141–155
Acoustic criteria
   See Features (Acoustic definition)
   See also Decoding
Active/passive 66, 71, 178, 180
Adjectival modification
   See Modification (Adjectival)
Adverbial modification
   See Modification (Adverbial)
Agreement 137–139
Alternations ix, 15f, 22ff, 30, 32, 186(9), 186(12)
   Classification of 32–38
Ambiguity 13, 73f, 184(15), 191(13)
Aphasia 13
Aquinas, T. 9
Archiphoneme 22, 37
   See also Neutralization
Armstrong, D. 195
Articulation
   See Encoding
Aspect
   See Russian (Aspect)
Attribution 117f, 119f, 120f, 122f
Autonomy
   Relative viii, 11, 16f, 22, 24, 39, 50, 173
   Of phonemics ix, 10f, 12ff, 18ff, 22, 25, 185(31)
   Of morphophonemics 12ff, 22, 25, 29ff, 32f, 39, 185(22), 186(12)
   Of syntax 172f
   See also Language and reality; Language and other spheres

Baudouin de Courtenay, J. 3, 9f, 36

Bloch, B. 17
Bloomfield, L. 186(9)
Bolinger, D. 119, 126, 178f, 191(2)
Bouma, L. 196
Bulgarian 19

Case
   See Russian (Declensional system)
Case grammar 163f
Caucasian languages 14
Chomsky, N. 17, 52, 122, 185(36)
Codes and sub-codes 21, 24
Competence/performance 66, 178ff
Conceptual features
   See Features (Conceptual)
Constitutent structure 173f
   See also Hierarchy (Of modification relations in syntax)
Contextual meaning
   See Meaning (General vs. contextual)
Cook, W. A. 196

Danish 20
Decoding 12ff, 16f, 21ff, 25, 28, 184(15)
Deep structure 6, 122, 171, 174ff
Deixis 107f, 109f, 115ff, 118f, 120, 125f, 147ff, 153, 155–162, 164f, 170, 171, 173ff
Derwing, B. 15f
Diachrony 37, 38, 161f
Dimensionality 80, 88f, 92f, 100–103, 152f, 166f, 170, 190(61)
Directionality
   See Extension
Distinctive features
   See Features (Distinctive)
Duplication 80, 100–103, 167

Encoding 12ff, 16f, 21ff, 25, 28, 29ff, 184(15)
English 21, 24, 33, 35, 68, 72, 73, 74, 75, 81, 82, 83, 85, 89, 94f, 114-119, 125f, 147, 151, 157, 161, 174, 175ff, 180, 190(62), 192(23), 193(28)
Extended meaning
  See Meaning (Extended)
  See also Stylistic variation
Extension 60f, 64, 67, 69f, 80, 87, 96, 98f, 100-103, 107f, 109, 135, 136, 145ff, 167f

Features
  Distinctive 4, 12, 16, 17, 18ff, 59, 63, 189(36)
  Redundant 21, 24
  Conceptual 60ff, 66f, 79f, 99-103, 104f, 133f, 141-155, 189(55)
  Distinctive 4, 12, 16, 17, 18ff, 21ff, 59, 63 189(36)
  Acoustic definition 3, 4, 25ff
  See also Opposition; Markedness
Ferguson, C. 16
Ferrell, J. 192(10)
Figurative meaning
  See Stylistic variation
  See also Metaphorical usage
Fillmore, C. 164, 196
Form
  See Meaning (As a function of form)
Formal determinism 7, 48f, 143, 180
  See also Meaning (As a function of form)
Forsyth, J. 192(8)
French 18f, 57, 72, 127-132, 177
Function
  See Meaning
  See also Teleology

Gardiner, D. 196
General meaning
  See Meaning (General vs. contextual)
German 63, 72
Gesamtbedeutung
  See Meaning (General vs. contextual)
Gestalt 56f
Government 63ff, 67, 133-137
Grammatical concepts 30f, 40ff, 43f, 54ff
Grammatical meaning 54-62, 105, 107, 157, 165, 172, 176, 180, 193(28)
  See also Russian

Grammatical prerequisites 12f, 22, 25, 30ff
  See also Encoding
Grammatical processes 30f, 43f
Grevisse, M. 196
Grundbedeutung
  See Meaning (General vs. contextual)

Haas, W. 179
Halle, M. 14ff, 22, 185(22)
Hierarchy
  Of levels in language viii, 11, 165, 172
  Of modification relations in syntax 113f, 122ff, 126f, 174
  Of conceptual features 148ff, 166ff
Holenstein, E. 61f, 75, 76, 183(1), 187(5), 188(26), 188(27), 189(46), 189(50), 189(51), 191(8)
Homonymy
  See Ambiguity
Howden, M. 197
Husserl, E. 61f

Iconicity 45, 187(21)
Idiolect 162
Intercatergorial invariance
  See Invariance (Intercategorial)
Interlingual invariance
  See Universals
Intracategorial invariance
  See Invariance (Intracategorial)
Invariance 47f, 52f, 57, 62-79, 141-155, 162, 188(19), 188(27)
  Topological/relational 18f, 52f, 54ff, 61f, 66f, 77f, 143ff, 188(29)
  Partial 77, 106
  Intracategorial 165
  Intercategorial 78, 79, 106f, 165, 189(55)
  Interlingual See Universals

Jakobson, R.
  On form and meaning 3ff, 29ff, 42f, 44f, 47f
  On topological/relational invariance 18ff, 54f, 61f, 144, 188(27)
  On teleology 26
  On relative autonomy 9ff, 12f
  On phonemics vs. morphophonemics 9ff, 12f, 17, 21ff, 25, 29ff, 35f, 184(15), 185(22), 185(31)
  On distinctive features 18ff, 21ff, 25ff, 68, 189(36)

On conceptual features 63, 67f, 68f, 72, 141f, 189(36)
On meaning and reference 49ff, 160f
On general and contextual meaning 53, 57
On Russian nominal inflection 42ff, 54–62, 64f, 79, 84, 96–99, 141f, 145ff, 165
On Russian verbal grammatical system 31f, 153
Johnson, D. B. 199

Kazan' school 9f
Kruszewski, M. 191(2)

Language and other spheres 10, 11, 56, 58, 185(36), 188(27)
See also Autonomy
Language and reality vii, 47f, 49ff, 65ff, 137, 156ff, 159ff, 164f, 179f
Levenberg, J. 170
Lexical meaning 104–111, 157–159, 165, 168, 172, 176
Lyons, J. 199

Marginality
See *Restrictedness*
Markedness relations
In phonology 62f, 68, 76
In morphology 63f, 68–77, 150, 152
In syntax 114f, 119, 120, 123ff, 127f
Reversals 75f
See also Opposition
Matejka, L. 6, 184(13)
Meaning
As a function of form vii, 3ff, 9ff, 29ff, 38f, 42f, 44f, 47f, 78, 95, 113f, 117f, 122, 137, 138f, 142f, 155f, 163ff, 171ff, 178f, 191(2)
As perception vii, 137, 144, 155–162, 164f, 166ff, 173ff, 179f
General vs. contextual 50ff, 53, 69ff, 71, 74, 75, 77, 92f, 116, 121, 179
In phonology 4, 9ff, 38f, 172
In morphology 3, 29ff, 40f, 42f, 44f, 47–111, 172
In syntax 4, 63ff, 113–139, 171–181
Extended meaning 72, 73; See also Stylistic variation
Metaphorical usage 128f, 191(13)
Modification 123ff
Adjectival 114–124, 127–131, 175f
Adverbial 124–127, 131f, 175f

Moscow school 36f

Neutralization 22f, 38, 63f, 67f, 133ff, 192(23)

Objectiveness 60f, 80, 100–103, 134f, 145ff, 151f, 154, 168
Old Church Slavic 170
Old Russian 170
Opposition 59ff, 62ff, 68ff, 116, 121, 128f, 133ff, 150ff
See also Features

Paradigmatic vs. syntagmatic relations 15, 24, 33ff, 70f, 113, 135, 146, 172ff
Parole
See Deixis
See also Competence/performance
Partial invariance
See Invariance (Partial)
Passive
See Active/passive
Peirce, C. S. 45, 53, 156
Perception
See Meaning (As perception)
See also Decoding
Perceptional deixis 107ff, 157ff, 165, 174, 175
Performance
See Competence/performance
Peškovskij, A. M. 55f
Phenomenology 61f, 122, 160, 188(26)
Phonemic overlapping 17f, 19ff, 66
Pos, H. J. 59
Prague school 22, 25, 26f, 63, 141, 186(12)
Predication 115f, 117f, 120f, 122f, 130f, 176f

Quantification
See *Objectiveness*
Questions, syntax of 176f

Ramage, E. xi
Redundancy 67f, 133ff, 137ff
See also Neutralization; Features (Redundant)
Redundant features
See Features (Redundant)
Reference 49ff, 56, 66f, 156f, 160f, 173f, 179f
See also Language and reality
Reformatskij, A. A. 36f

Relational invariance
  See Invariance (Topological/relational)
Relative autonomy
  See Autonomy (Relative)
Relativity
  See Invariance (Topological/relational)
Restrictedness 60f, 64f, 67, 70, 76, 80–99,
  100–103, 108, 110, 145ff, 151, 153,
  158f, 168, 190(62)
Rozental', D. E. 120
Russian ix, 24, 33, 34, 35, 72, 161, 166,
  180
  Agreement, 137–139
  Aspect 91ff, 152ff, 166f
  Declensional system' 42, 44f, 54–62,
    69–71, 75f, 95–99, 144–150, 167,
    168
  Preposition/preverb system 79–95,
    99–104, 167f
  Syntax 117f, 119–125, 133–139, 177
  Tense system 150–155, 168
  Verbal and prepositional government
    64ff, 67, 133–137
  Verbal grammatical morphology 31f,
    36f, 39–42
  Verbal lexicon 106–110, 157–159,
    168
  Voicing in obstruent clusters 15f, 22

Sangster, R. 183(1), 188(26), 191(12)
Sapir, E. 30
Saussure, F. de 3, 5, 26, 63
Šaxmatov, A. A. 120
Semantic coefficient 169ff, 192(18)
Semantic compatibility/incompatibility
  64, 75, 76f, 95f, 116, 132, 134
Semantic dominant
  See Semantic coefficient
Semantic features
  See Features (Conceptual)
  See also *Dimensionality; Duplication;*
    Extension; Objectiveness;
    Restrictedness; Transitivity
Semantic overlapping 66f, 71, 179
Semiotics 4, 9, 11, 47 50, 185(36)
Sense determination
  See Encoding
Sense discrimination
  See Decoding
Serbo-Croatian 169f
Speech event
  See Deixis

Speech perception
  See Decoding
Speech production
  See Encoding
Sphota 9
Stankiewicz, E. 36, 41, 186(12)
Steiner, G. 200
Structuralism viii, ix, 22, 160
Stylistic variation 72, 73, 99, 117f, 121,
  124f, 172
Sweet, H. 10
Synonymy 65f, 178
Syntagmatic relations
  See Paradigmatic vs. syntagmatic
    relations
  See also Syntax
Syntax 4, 63ff, 113–139, 171–181

Tag questions 177
Teleology 25f
Tense
  See Russian (Tense system)
Topology
  See Invariance (Topological/relational)
Townsend, C. xi
Transformational-generative grammar 22,
  174f, 192(23)
Transmissional deixis 107f, 157, 165,
  175ff, 192(23), 193(28)
  See also Deixis
Transitivity 108f, 159, 166, 192(16)
Trubetzkoy, N. 36
Truth value 51, 160, 180
Turkish 16

Universals 79, 95, 163–171
Unmarked 68ff, 73f, 179, 191(13)
  See also Markedness relations; Oppo-
    sition

Van Schooneveld, C. H. vii, x, xi, 62, 78,
  79, 85, 88, 90, 91, 98, 99ff, 107, 110,
  120, 122, 123f, 134f, 145, 146ff, 154,
  165, 166ff, 169, 186(10), 189(55),
  190(61), 191(9), 192(16), 192(22)
Verifiability 145–155, 164
  See also Invariance (Intercategorial)
Vinogradov, V. V. 188(24)
Voicing
  See Russian (Voicing in obstruent
    clusters)

Waugh, L. xi, 27, 189(48), 189(49), 191(12)
Weinreich, U. 141f

Word order
See Modification